9-

Terra Infirma

BOOKS BY
Rodger Kamenetz

Nonfiction

The Jew in the Lotus

Stalking Elijah

Poetry

The Missing Jew:
New and Selected Poems

Nymphology

Stuck

Rodger Kamenetz

Terra
Infirma

A MEMOIR OF MY
MOTHER'S LIFE IN MINE

SCHOCKEN BOOKS   NEW YORK

All rights reserved under International and Pan-American
Copyright Conventions. Published in the United States
by Schocken Books Inc., New York, and simultaneously in
Canada by Random House of Canada Limited, Toronto.
Distributed by Pantheon Books, a division of Random House,
 Inc., New York. Originally published in the United States
by The University of Arkansas Press, Fayetteville, in 1985.

SCHOCKEN and colophon are trademarks of Schocken Books Inc.

Library of Congress Cataloging-in-Publication Data
Kamenetz, Rodger, 1950-
Terra infirma : a memoir of my mother's life in mine / Rodger Kamenetz.
p. cm.
Originally published: Fayetteville : University of Arkansas Press, c1985.
ISBN 0-8052-4167-1
1. Kamenetz, Rodger, 1950-   —Family.
2. Poets, American—20th century—Family relationships.
3. Mothers and sons—United States.
4. Kamenetz, Miriam. I. Title.
PS3561.A4172Z477 1999 811'.54—dc21 98-19276 [b] CIP

Random House Web Address: www.randomhouse.com
Printed in the United States of America
9 8 7 6 5 4 3 2 1

For my family

Acknowledgments

Parts of *Terra Infirma* have previously appeared in slightly different forms in the following publications: *Baltimore Sun, Exquisite Corpse, Grand Street, Jewish Times, Missouri Review, North American Review*, and *Shenandoah*.

I have used brief quotations from the following works: Malcolm de Chazal, *Sens Plastique*, trans. Irving Weiss (*New York Sun*, 1979); Robert Duncan, *The Opening of the Field* (New York: Grove Press, 1960); Lucretius, *On the Nature of Things*, trans. Cyril Bailey (Oxford: Clarendon Press, 1910); Frank O'Hara, *Selected Poems*, ed. Donald Allen (New York: Vintage Books, 1974); *Selections from the Essays of Montaigne*, trans. Donald Frame (New York: Appleton-Century Crofts, 1948).

Contents

Terra Infirma

a beginning

My mother died in the Church Home Hospice in Balti-more, at the age of 54. Her last words were "I love you." The radio was playing "Raindrops Keep Falling on My Head." The immediate cause was respiratory infection, a complication of prolonged medication for pain. My mother suffered cancer for seven years. At the end, a nurse stripped the neck brace, pressed her fingers against the carotid ar-tery, and felt for the faintest sign of a pulse. The velcro made a sound like stitches ripping.

I remember the moment of her death, and in the mo-ments that followed, a kind of wonder at myself, in my own blind efficiency. My father sat stunned as though this weren't something we had anticipated all along. I called my two sisters, and my two brothers, and told them to come downtown and see our mother's body. I called the fu-neral home, Sol Levinson Brothers. I remember looking them up in the yellow pages, which seemed odd. Shouldn't there be a card, or something, in a hospice? I had all these thoughts. All these practical, cold, abstracted thoughts. Because my mother was dead, and someone had to do something, and I was there to do it.

I felt very responsible for everything that happened. I felt

1

responsible and guilty. I had needed to be there at the moment she died. I was calling the funeral home, and saying "My mother is dead" and saying "Her name is Miriam Kamenetz," and giving a date, an address and a time. All along my mother's body was lying on the bed in the dim lamplight. Her face was crumpled and had lost all its quality. It looked like a rubber mask tossed off on the pillow.

For the next week, I simply rode along on my feeling of mission. The funeral, and the seven days of mourning, coming together with my family, comforting one another, and through all of it, I saw that my eyes were open, and I was observing very carefully, like a son of a bitch, like a writer. I was not cold. I was feeling everything. But back there, way back, I was pivoting around, and seeing, and noting, and remembering.

I knew I had witnessed something extraordinary at the instant of her death. Her last gesture had moved right into me. It was staying with me all through the mourning, there in the place from which I am writing this down.

But I could not put it on paper then. It seemed a violation. I could see her whole life gathering around her last moment. I felt that I could hold its pattern in my hand. But then the fabric would dissolve and I had the gesture of lifting a wave out of water.

I thought I had to let her story go. But three dreams came in the months after she died. They came to disturb, but also to comfort. In the third, very elaborate vision, my mother appeared in a garden to give me a key to her story. I had to write about her then. Just as soon as I began, the dreams stopped.

All the same, I was afraid it would be too sentimental. For what story is more sentimental than the death of a boy's mother—even though Edgar Poe, for one, called it the most "poetical" of subjects? Poe also promised immortality to the author who wrote a simple volume, "My Heart Laid Bare." As though a naive writer could triumph over all the artifices of a master, if only he were sufficiently earnest. But Poe added puckishly, "The title must be true to its subject."

Here is such a volume. But I can be true to the subject only by straying from it. I have read a few books that have been more dutiful. They were all published by the vanity press. Like mine, they were haunted by the loss of a loved one. But their authors make no distinction between history and poetry, as Aristotle does. They tell every detail, in chronological order, as though the reader already acknowledged their significance. They do not see that, at best, history aggregates, only poetry unifies.

I wish to lay my heart bare. But my model is complex, the essay in its radical sense, as practiced by Michel de Montaigne. I admire him because he is so artful there is nothing he cannot say.

Here I must digress, to speak of Montaigne's digression. Only someone constantly aware of his subject could digress so freely. The revelation is always present, not as in the ordinary magic of suspense—but as a barely visible tracing, a pattern of avoidance.

Aggressive writing pursues its subject—a hunting metaphor. Digressive writing flees a painful absence—a haunting metaphor. For Montaigne the hollow induced skepticism, of which digression carved out a warning. For me, the haunting is literal: the dream that comes after death.

Montaigne's project is not always what it seems. If he titles a piece "On Coaches," his subject is not coaches. The title is more like a sign hung outside his construction—WRITING AT WORK. An aggressive reader chasing after the subject, coaches, is quickly outpaced. The coaches disappear at the first or second turn of phrase, and the more determinedly the reader pursues the supposed "subject,"

3

the more exhausted he becomes, and the more empty the page feels. He has been abandoned by "coaches" and does not yet feel the writing as its own vehicle of transportation. If he lets himself be moved by the prose instead of pursuing the "coaches," then he begins to feel a profound absence of connections and is deeply in Montaigne's skepticism.

I cannot promise that my material is uplifting either. The subject here is death and grief. I am sorry for that, more sorry perhaps than any reader. If I had seen where it would lead me, I might have resisted more strongly. For I have discovered something, apart from the ordinary cynicism that "no one wants to read about death." The subject repulses thought.

Each time I approached the core of feeling around my mother's death, I found my thinking diverted. At first I accused myself of a lack of discipline, or a simple avoidance. I am now convinced, though, that this was at least a complex avoidance. My digression is language turning in grief. Turning away from its subject, to approach it again. This makes for a labyrinthine or spiraling pattern.

This book is part memoir, part biography of my mother, part autobiography. But neither my mother nor I are celebrities. We never committed great crimes. She was entirely a private person, and I am a poet in America, which is the opposite of fame. Yet the pattern of every life is instructive, and an ordinary death may be as tragic as *Oedipus*.

Every day others will reach the point my mother reached. They will be given terrible medical choices, cures that seem worse than the disease. Many will make courageous decisions as my mother did. I wish this story could be an inspiring one for them, about how defiance won the day, how the doctors were proven wrong, how a fighting spirit confounded science. Some popular books about death have this theme. My mother's story offers no hope. Her defiance did not win in the end.

Yet, if she had read the book of her life, she might have lived. If she had been able to digress, to step away from her own story, she might have seen herself as more than just a body in danger, when she had to decide whether to live or die. Her story, I have come to believe, is tragic. But I did not see this pattern immediately. At the beginning I had only the pain at her death, and three vivid dreams.

1

on dreams

In 1980, at the height of the gold boom, my grandfather came to give advice. His advice was a silent gesture, and so, subject to interpretation. Visualize him: a short feisty man, a silver-haired bantam. "You have to dress like a businessman," he would say, rushing the word *businessman* with great hustle and bustle so that all the *s*'s seemed to shake at once. He was a dry cleaner. His clothes were spotless.

Of twenty grandchildren, only one listened. He became a doctor. Like the Pierce-Arrow, chocolate soda, and Chinese cabbages, his investments in advice had a high failure rate. Now that he is dead, he gives advice in dreams.

Dream advice seems more authoritative. But it's vaguer. At times I interpret dreams psychologically, at times mystically, but I prefer the school of Joseph. I like the directness: seven fat cattle, seven years of plenty; seven lean cattle, seven years of famine. My dreams, too, have streamlined: simple decor, easy symbols, clear plot line.

When I was eighteen years old and had nothing to write about, I began to write down my dreams. At first they cooperated, short and sweet, clear lovely haiku. But soon my pen was tested by the picaresque, spiky plots with odd characters. Woody Allen would usher in a trembling Richard Nixon who would take me out for a hamburger while the dream took me nowhere. Impossible to interpret, and damned difficult to write down. Still, I persisted.

Then a peculiar thing. Consciously I entered my dreams as though I were taking notes inside them. Psychologists call this lucid dreaming. But for me, it was the dream equivalent of suicide. I was driving uphill. I said, "This is just a dream. I can do anything I want. I can take this car and drive it into the wall." I was driving, indeed, on a street from my childhood, Liberty Road. So I was going to steer that dream at liberty, that is, towards the wall. I grabbed the wheel and turned, but it didn't budge. Some force of equal strength to my own seemed to be fighting against me. The animal part of my will pushed from the other end of the steering column as if the body of the car were fighting the mind of the driver. Finally, with great force, I yanked the car, not into the wall, but over the yellow line. I was now speeding up the wrong side of Liberty with an Exxon truck barreling down upon me. I woke before the crash. I took this as a warning to stop writing my dreams.

As a child I used to dream of falling and always wake before I landed. I had stolen a car. And they were after me. Just *they*. The owners, the parents, the owners of the world. I had raced the car as fast as I could and finally, crashing through a barrier, the car fell. I would be falling now in space, the car evaporated, falling towards the reservoir, the canyon, the junkyard, the river, the black pit forever. I never landed. If I did, I knew I would die.

That absolute fear has never left me. But it has been made to stand in a corner. I have chastened my dreams, taught them a Biblical sternness and simplicity, values I associate with my grandfather. So I was particularly shocked by his specter. True, he was neat as ever. He was wearing a blue shortsleeve shirt, wash and wear, a shirt I had appropriated from his dresser drawer the day he was buried. (I also slept in his bed that night.) What shocked me was the necklace. My grandfather would no more wear one than Harry Truman, whom he closely resembled in old age. A pimp's necklace: large gold nuggets. Rays of light emanated from each chunk in a nimbus. My grandfather's finger had also changed. It was coy and elegant, almost feminine, not gnarled and arthritic. It pointed back to the glowing necklace.

"What are you trying to tell me?" I asked. I am a blunt dreamer. In answer, my grandfather stretched his lips and revealed a set of teeth, all gold.

At first, following the school of Joseph, I was simple enough to believe the dream meant I should buy gold. But I couldn't act on a dream. That seemed as fierce a penetration of my life as my attempt to crash the car had been of my dreams.

Anyway, why should his advice be any better now that he is dead? The dead are no wiser than they were in life, although they are surer. I do believe they come back if you make a place for them.

In Mexico, I saw some personal shrines for the dead in a friend's home. Photographs framed in gilt with a black curtain, a drawstring and a handwritten prayer. I have no such shrine. I have a yellowed photograph with a date scribbled in pencil across the back. It is a photo of my mother in 1959 when I was nine years old. She is smiling and that tells you nothing.

Still, when she comes back in a dream, she comes through that photograph. It is her medium. Out of this still shot in black and white, she steps forward in color and three dimensions.

The first time my mother came, I nearly drove her away with my bluntness. I met her at a party. It was one of her terrific parties of the fifties, when everyone was loud and joyous and seemed to be honking and laughing at once. My mother collected people: down-and-out artists, beatniks, insurance salesmen, pharmacists, neighbors, friends, no relatives. She'd mix them up and watch them bounce off each other.

I'd stay up as late as I could. The men would flirt with each other's wives or tell loud jokes in the corner of the living room. The women would hustle back and forth to the kitchen or bathroom, heavy rouge, perfume, low-cut dresses. Just middle-class people, but animated. I didn't know what drinking was, but it seemed magical. What was pumping through them that made them—bigger.

My father was even smoking cigarettes. He smoked them out of little sample packs of Winstons he got from the drugstore. He mixed a drink called an old-fashioned: dark and thick as furniture polish and brown, with an orange peel stuck on the rim. In the morning I'd get up early, sample the empty drinks that were scattered about: on the piano, floor, TV, cabinets. I'd sip the flat pop. I'd eat the maraschino cherries and lick the onion dip off my fingers. The after-party mood was subdued. I felt like an explorer coming upon the scene of a great and foreign disaster. A hurricane had swirled through the house, but I didn't understand the nature of the storm, why Mr. Kovaleski was looking at Mrs. Sachs that way, why there was a fist-fight in the kitchen, why they had to call a cab for Benny Freeman. It had something to do with the old-fashioned, but when I tasted it in the morning, I spit it out. It was just bitter.

My mother would dress herself for such a party in something trim and fashionable. In the fifties, her hair was still loose, dark and wavy. Her dress was red and low-necked. She wore black stack heels of patent leather and rouge on her cheeks. Her bright red lipstick made her smile a bite.

As I came up to her, she was in the middle of a group of friends, had just finished laughing and now her laugh was dropping back. "But Mom," I said, breaking into the group, "What are you doing here? You're dead."

Just stupid blunt, that's all. She looked right past me, didn't skip a beat, as if to say, "fool."

Interpreting that dream seemed so simple at the time. I was having trouble accepting deeply that my mother was dead. Consciously, I knew she was, but the rest of me thought she wasn't. Fine enough. Only now I have come to ask myself, which part was correct?

"But Mom, you're dead." My bluntness. But she wasn't. She was alive, and her putdown, the way she bulled ahead as if my remark were just another foolish drip from my lips, that was *her* way. Not mine.

It was several weeks later before she would bother to appear again. I was upset to see her and apologized for not getting her a birthday present. She told me that the dead hang out at the synagogues to hear Kaddish prayers, and I felt ashamed because I had not been praying Kaddish.

People say in soothing tones that in such dreams you learn to "accept" death. I don't like that phrase, "accept death." Is death acceptable?

I don't know. I have a dream in which my grandfather told me that no one lives alone or ever dies alone. He told me this after he died. He also told me that when I was in a happy mood, my voice seemed bright to him like "sunlight on a ditch." But he said he could see my sad words fall off "the curve of the earth."

My mother also brought me an answer. I dreamed it in Roberval in northern Quebec, the nearest I've ever been to the Arctic Circle. It was the day of the summer solstice, two months after she died. My motel room had photo-wallpaper of a Canadian landscape: bright orange, trees and a lake. Even with the lights off, it glowed. It reminded me of a rug my mother had placed in our living room when I was thirteen. That rug was bright orange too, a fuzzy round shag. It sat on a floor of dark mahogany that made it vibrate. I'd stare until it lost all color. I'd close my eyes and see a dark blue rug on a white floor, its ghost equivalent. That rug had a history. It was blunt too, like me, like my mother, like a slap in the face.

It could not get dark in Roberval on the longest day of the year. Midnight looked like four P.M. I tossed and stared at the orange wallpaper and didn't fall asleep until dawn.

Her visit this time was so calm and regal, I no longer cared for interpretations. The dream had authority, its own manner of speaking. I'd no more quarrel with it than with an apple.

My mother and I were walking in a French garden, a careful neat garden with fountains at intervals. We were silent, as though under a spell of enchantment, one of those moments that comes sometimes at the end of a long afternoon of walking and talking on a perfect fall day. We stopped and looked back along the way we had come. A goldfish splashed in the water, an oriole flew from an apple branch, a coin dropped on the tile edge of the fountain. Three events, one after the other. A voice, which seemed to be coming from everywhere at once, said, "All these things pass through the spirit like a single wave through water."

I took this to mean that the three events that had just occurred, though apparently distinct, were actually part of a single motion like a wave. And that my mother came from a place where you could see the wave. Then the voice added, "There are two voices. One is continuous and belongs to both of us. The other . . ." I woke with the sensation that "the voice" speaking with such deep authority was my own.

11

I remember waking from that dream with great joy. I carefully copied all the details in a small black notebook I'd laid on the night table beside me.

I was enough in the school of Joseph to believe the dream promised me a key—a way of pulling together the scattered events of my mother's life. I knew now that I had to write about her.

Yet, I was enough in the school of Freud to suspect the dream was my own mind, comforting itself.

2

cerebellar poetry

The mind makes its own opium. The opiate receptors in the brain exist to receive an anodyne from the brain itself. The mind is self-sufficient. We make our own solace. The mind provides for itself out of itself, relieves pain and allows sleep by making whole what was partial and painful.

Lucretius, who wrote "on the nature of things," thought the mind must be something like a pile of poppy seeds. I love antique science, as calm and self-assured as today's, but richly metaphoric and instructively wrong. The mind, Lucretius tells us, "is very fine in texture and is made and formed of very tiny particles." His proof? "Nothing is seen to come to pass so swiftly as what the mind pictures to itself coming to pass and starts to do itself. The mind stirs itself more quickly than the things that stir. But because it is so very nimble, it is bound to be formed of exceeding round and exceeding tiny seeds, so that its particles may be able to move when smitten by a little impulse. Just so, a light trembling breath can scatter a high heap of poppy seeds before your eyes . . ."

The "voice" in my dream had come to speak of the mind. It told me that an idea is really a single wave that moves through the brain, setting off trains of transient

13

lights, details that glimmer, like the oriole, the penny, and the splash in my dream. They are all one movement. It is all one, any idea, a whole, and we only spit out part of it in expression, break it off into articulated bits, words, images, pictures, moments: the whole pile of poppy seeds ripples and shimmers, ruffled by a breath.

My mother came in a dream to tell me about my mind which was appropriate since she had landscaped so much of it. That is why we strolled through a French garden: orderly and geometric.

The last moments I could talk to my mother, and get a response, we spent in a garden. She was in a high-back wheelchair with tiny wheels. The pain in her spine, even with the morphine, was so bad that the seams in the floor made her wince. When it came time to roll over the copper sill to take us outside, I agonized but I could not spare her the jolt. Her face tightened and she yelped; tears flew from her eyes. Two inches of metal but the small wheels were stuck and I could not get her over. Damn it, damn her, damn everything, I pushed it, not so much for her as for myself; I couldn't stand her stuck and hopeless, one set of wheels into the garden.

"Mom, are you all right?"

Tears streamed down her face. I gave her time to compose herself, then wheeled her down the path.

"Look at the white tulips, Mom."

"They're pretty." They were the first words she had said to anyone since her long silence had begun. They were the last words she said to me. I felt this satisfaction: she had seen them. And they were pretty: white tulips in a hospice garden.

I suppose this event is what Freud would call the dream-substrate in his oddly chemical terminology. And it is a strange chemistry that metabolizes a plot of white tulips into a French garden, that distills a painful reality into a dream and then gives the dream back to soothe the reality. "These things," the voice said, "seem separate, but they pass through the spirit in a single wave." Nothing is separate, nothing can be taken from you, the voice was saying, not your mother, not me . . .

If we spend a third of our lives asleep and a quarter of that time dreaming, that means we spend two hours out of every twenty-four locked in a dream. Why do we dream so much and so long? Over a lifetime, there are five years of solid dreaming. Five years: a childhood of dreaming, a college of dreams.

Dreaming begins in the womb. The eyes of the fetus can be seen moving rapidly, and it is believed the brain matures through dreaming, that dreams provide stimulus in the darkness of the womb. Inside a mother each of us begins a dream.

The other day, lying in bed, I felt my heart beating for the first time in a long while. I realized how little I live in my body, how much in my mind. My arms could fall off and I might not notice. I'm all head like a jellyfish, and my body is thin, membraneous, trailing off vaguely in the waters.

I was reading Lucretius and was struck by the ancient poet's assurance as he asserted that all thoughts emanate from the chest. "The head and lord in the whole body is the middle region of the breast." His reason? "For here it is that fear and terror throb, around these parts are soothing joys; here then is the understanding and the mind."

It seems odd that whole nations of men lived believing that their thoughts came from somewhere between their armpits and their chins. I can't locate my thoughts there, try as I might. I know they come from behind my forehead.

Odd imperialism of the body that gives so much dominance to the head. I've even thought I could locate the origin of some idea the way a sufferer might locate a headache. The back of the brain is the place for deep gorgeous dark ideas—the front for nimble calculations, piano arpeggios and quick flights of light. This topography seems as real to me as Lucretius's did to him.

But where do ideas come from? They must pass through my whole body like the wave "the voice" spoke of in my dream. Or they rise up slowly in fumes from the feet, calves, genitals, bowels, only to precipitate in the brain pan.

This is about as scientific as Lucretius. It is the only science I care to do. I want a certain kind of truth; I want to see things as they are for me. When Montaigne tells us he had his sleep disturbed by servants, "so that I might catch a glimpse of it," I laugh but I applaud the impulse.

There is a special seeing that arises in delight and leads to refreshment, that enters the mind through the body and ends in the embodiment of knowledge. What we know of the world becomes a part of our bodies. "When I dance, I dance," writes Montaigne, "when I sleep, I sleep; yes, and when I walk alone in a beautiful orchard, if my thoughts have been concerned with extraneous incidents for some part of the time, for some other part I lead them back again to the walk, to the orchard, to the sweetness of this solitude, and to myself." So I walked in a garden with my mother, and in the garden of my dream. And Montaigne tells us Nature has observed this principle "in a *motherly* fashion . . . that the actions she has enjoined on us for our need should also give us pleasure."

Each body, properly seen, gives its beauty. We know it sometimes on the beach when all these pasty, burnt, hairy and nearly naked bodies are awash across canvas colored sand. I have experienced it also in museums. Once, in the Louvre, after hours of statue gazing in the antiquities section, I began looking at the museum-goers with the same ardor. The results were astonishing and sexy. Their clothes fell away and I was surrounded by walking classical art.

I have experienced similar revelations while extremely tired. Mostly, then, I notice faces. Each face so perfectly genuine, perfectly itself. Which sounds perfectly meaningless—except there is a quality to reality when I am exhausted: it no longer seems "photographed" but "painted" —and therefore much more *intended*. This feeling of intention—as if someone had put every face there for my personal appreciation—is the closest I have ever come to a mystical experience.

In the same way I saw those tulips. They leaped out at me, they were outlined by the grave facts that surrounded them and made them important: they were to be my mother's last sight, my last gift to her. That much is obvious. But what made them strange was how much they belonged to her, belonged to her death. It was their color in that late afternoon light. They had an odd silvery transparency like the deadly Amanita mushroom, the White Angel. They were like nothing I had ever seen on this earth. They were ready to be taken with her.

My mother's malady involved a part of the brain I had never located in my imaginings. I knew little about it then but have since come to know it well. The cerebellum—the little brain—is in the back of the head. If I cup my hand and place my palm just above the back of my neck I can find it, gray and mushy, folded even more than the cerebral cortex. In evolutionary terms, the cerebellum is very old. It evolved in primitive reptiles as a lump riding the top of the spinal cord. In mammals, it folded, striated, became more capable in its functions. It was the first part of the brain to specialize, to become something in itself.

The "little brain" is humble. It does not share in the glories of the cerebral cortex, the seat of thought. Neither is it a source, like the midbrain, for deep trains of images. No dreaming is done in the cerebellum. Its role in the brain is analogous to my mother's role in our family; it functions,

17

the textbook tells us, "to coordinate, adjust and smooth out movements."

When I reach for a cup of coffee, the idea comes from the cerebrum. But as the impulse is passed to my hand, a duplicate message goes to the cerebellum and, likewise, as my hand moves towards the cup, it reports on its progress to both the cerebrum and the cerebellum. The cerebellum compares messages and decides whether any adjustment needs to be made. It sends signals to smooth out the movement and bring my hand to a halt at the cup.

If my cerebellum is damaged, when my hand moves toward the cup, no feedback signal is received. My cerebrum takes over, tells the arm that it is moving too far too fast, and pushes it back a little. But the cerebrum is clumsy in its work. Its ideas are perhaps too general, it doesn't appreciate the finer things in life. My hand oscillates, overshooting its mark, then undershooting the adjustment. The result is what the doctors call an intention tremor, a sure sign of cerebellar damage. The hands shake with intention, though they are normal at rest.

Malcolm de Chazal, an African writer, wrote that "in the true poet, the cerebrum is a lyre played by the cerebellum." The poet shapes his brain into a lyre; he harmonizes it as a sensitive instrument, tuned to receive the shocks of life, as I received the sight of those white tulips. He does not write, as others write, to "express ideas," but builds his mind into a lyre, a harmony of tones and pitches, light and dark, ready to be played.

The cerebellum is the fit musician. Through countless gestures of the body, it learns every nuance of desire. It remembers the delicacy of every graceful gesture, and the exact movements of pain, how my arms felt, for instance, pushing my mother's wheelchair over the sill.

The cerebellum plays the cerebrum because it has the necessary lightness of touch. The "sensual music" of all

18

good poetry is a harmony of body and mind. Poetry is not purely cerebral. Its soul is the body.

My mother's dream had the wholeness I felt in poetry. It restored what had been torn, united what had been separated. In sickness, her body and mind had been separated by the cruel attack on her cerebellum. But in the dream, her mind and body were restored, just as nature and reason joined in the formal garden. Most of all, mother and son were together again.

I'd had a vision, for a vision can be defined as highly articulate dreaming. My mother had come in a garden to give me a key to my story—and hers. I knew, from then on, I had to write about her. But how could I begin? What was the spirit the dream spoke of? What poetry could unite the dispersed events of any person's life?

I did not know what pattern I would find, though eventually I came to see how my mother's story was a tragedy, even a classical tragedy—complete with tragic flaw and a heroine who did not know herself. But at the beginning, I did not know this.

I was simply searching for essential memories, wandering through my house, trying to think of some way to begin. Then I saw an object that seemed to radiate my mother's spirit.

3

the piano

The piano, a Gulbransen spinet, fruitwood, three metal pedals, eighty-eight keys of white and black, sits in a living room in a rented house in Baton Rouge.

It is my piano in the living room of the house I rent. We have both arrived through a mysterious agency, in a spasmodic motion, as if my fate were a clanky steam-driven device. Another man's fate might hum like a computer. Mine lies dormant for years, jerks into action, and sends me and my piano whirling a thousand miles into space.

The piano was the only regular inheritance from my mother. It is mine like most things in my family, by virtue of forebearance. My sisters wanted it more, but I deserved it through long-suffering and took it as my due. I have the affection for that piano a monk might have for his hair shirt.

The piano too has suffered. It had no desire to be part of my mother's legacy or to come into my possession, just as in its early life, it had no desire to punish members of my family. Now it has suffered at all of our hands. Every octave has permanently depressed keys. They give this rather prim spinet a faintly obscene air, like a subway poster with blackened teeth. As my brother and I rolled it up to the U-HAUL on its dainty wheels, it cracked under one leg.

For most of its useful life, the piano sat unused. It made a splendid piece of furniture, a sleek platform of polished wood for photographs of all the children who never learned to play it. When I visited, I would lift the bench door and raise Clementi from the dead. After I was living on my own, I often asked my mother if I could have the piano. I thought I would take up where I had left off, somewhere just beyond the Bach Inventions and the Czerny School of Velocity. That name appealed to me. I pictured Czerny, a Czech with moustaches, on rollerskates, barrelling at high speed while Mr. Kracko, my piano teacher, played a rollicking rollerrink scherzo.

I told my mother once that her new home was sterile. She never forgave me for that remark, which I made in a fit of pique. I read once that Bob Dylan bought the house he lived in as a boy, just so he could return on occasion to live in his old room. I understand the sentiment and if I had the money I'd do the same. My mother's new home was sterile for me. It had no memories. Memories stay in a house you leave behind. The new owners have to live among your old memories. To leave the piano unplayed only compounded the problem. I hated it being so useless. I wanted to take it to my new bare apartment downtown and play it loud. My mother told me she thought the living room would look empty without it.

My mother always wanted me to play the piano. She had started with my sisters after they had given up on ballet. One day there was a piano and the next day, or very soon after, there was a young woman, Mrs. Peabody, who taught them to play. Somehow my sisters managed to get out of it, by growing breasts I think. It was no longer so important to teach them scales. So the bench they barely warmed was passed on to me.

The spinet was the first thing you saw as you walked into our old house. At first I liked it. I learned all about CDE, who had a tree, full of apples as can be; about CDE's friend, CBA, and very soon after I learned that every good boy does fine—presumably if he looks out the window into the pasture, where he can see that all cows eat grass. I liked whole notes, round eggs that sat on their shelves and spelled F,A,C,E. But these mnemonics were toys.

The serious duet was between my mother and me. The piano was a guilt-harp and she played beautifully. "I paid for this piano," went the chorus, "and you're going to practice it." My feelings were mixed. Sometimes I would sit for hours, practicing, playing, really enjoying it. My mother would say, "Play for me, Rod," using the most tender nickname. She had no favorite pieces, but in dynamics, she preferred *pianissimo* to *forte*.

We never had a functioning record player in the house until I was a teenager. My father's only avowed musical preference was for the 1812 Overture. Still, ours was a musical household. I mean by that only that a silent, unexpressed music resided somewhere in the vicinity of my mother. This melancholy music I inherited, like the piano, but it was never formally passed on. It came outside my lessons.

I never relished the mechanics of notes and duration, but like my mother, had a feel for dynamics. Often I would sit in the dark and let my fingers wander abstractedly, improvising odd melodies that seemed closer to the dreamy inner music I wanted to reach. I didn't know then that there was a real world of music that might have fulfilled me, that somewhere a composer had dreamed my dreams, clarified them, and taken them far beyond anything I could have imagined. We had no music in the house of that order. I never reached the proficiency in playing to reach it either. Instead I played scaled down versions of "The

22

Flight of the Bumblebee," "The Spinning Wheel," and a particularly lugubrious piece that seemed to be about dying fowl called "The Great Heron of the Everglades." Real music was beyond my reach, part of the world of culture and refinement my mother aspired to, though the details were sketchy. I was to be her emissary there. But as a child, I certainly did not understand the urgency of her insistence that I practice, or how that was linked to her own disastrous childhood. I was stubborn and lazy.

The duet went on for years, my mother's pushing, my resisting even what was clearly "good for me," resisting finally because to do otherwise was to give up a part of myself I needed, my dumb animal will. The result was a comical stalemate. Mr. Kracko, an Ichabod Crane who lived with his sister, would sit in the church room where I had my Saturday lessons, unaware of the dramas of the evening before. His fingers were so long and joints so knobby that I never doubted him when he told me a good pianist could do push-ups on his fingertips.

He told my mother once I was his favorite pupil. If so, I feel sorry for him. I have no idea what made him endure the weekly charade, when, after I stumbled through a piece, he would play the offended passage for me, then turn and ask, as sternly as was possible to him, "Did you practice every day this week?" I either had not practiced at all, or practiced once, furiously, the night before, my mother screaming, "What am I wasting money on you for, you *shtonk*? Do you think I need to take you every Saturday—I don't have better things to do?" and feeling like the furtive ingrate I was, I'd rush to the piano bench and hammer scales, *molte fortissimo*, hoping to drown my mother's voice as she asked, "Do you want to stop playing piano?" and "Yes" I felt like screaming back, but I'd shake my head no, just as I'd lie again the next day to Mr. Kracko, "Oh, I did practice some."

23

I remember that the day I left for college my mother's parting words were, "Don't forget to practice the piano." I promised.

Years later, as I left Baltimore for Louisiana, I remembered that broken promise, and several others, and so rented a truck to take the piano with me.

A U-HAUL truck is an unlovely thing to park outside a cemetery. But I had no choice. There simply was going to be no other time to visit my mother's grave. I walked through the archway of the gatehouse and passed the high kitsch monument dedicated to the Silver family and then walked down among the more homely middle-class gravestones to the Kamenetz graves. People who say cemeteries are peaceful probably have no means of reception for the powerful static of rushing voices that throb there. I don't believe all cemetery visits can be fruitful because there is no reason why, once having discarded the body, the soul should haunt its remains. My belief is that simply as a matter of tact and convenience, some souls make an effort from time to time to be present at a common meeting place. This is what I prefer to imagine when I believe there is a soul at all.

I was in something of a mood though. The U-HAUL truck was parked at a forty-five degree angle, two wheels on the grass. I felt similarly precarious. I was going to Louisiana with a piano in my truck, not a banjo on my knee. I was leaving Baltimore, all my family and friends and my mother's grave. I wanted to leave a forwarding address.

"I'm going to Louisiana," I stated bluntly, standing in front of her grave. I felt silly. If the soul is as I imagine it, it really doesn't matter if you say things out loud or not. I picked up a pebble, the largest I could find, and placed it on her gravestone. It is a Jewish custom to leave this calling card. A useful one, actually. A stone was already on her grave. Aunt Rachel must have left it. She was deeply re-

24

ligious and it would be like her to be more devoted to mother in death than she'd been in life. No one else had visited in a long time.

I stood for a few more minutes, making my mind a blank, thinking superstitiously that some message or feeling would wash over me if I made myself receptive. Nothing.

I got to Louisiana in two days of manic driving, but I'm afraid I left my soul behind. It happened Louisiana's tourist slogan was "the dream state." That described my state as well. There were no borders between me and my past life. I still believed I could call my best friend and go over for a beer. The call was three dollars and the friend was a thousand miles away.

I traveled those thousand miles in the U-HAUL truck, bouncing along in the August heat, watching a maniac with a swaying boat trailer cut me off in North Carolina; cringing in Mississippi while an EXTRA WIDE jockeyed lanes like a sports car. When I finally was able to pass him, a sunburned Elvis Presley with a duckass haircut lifted a can of Dixie Beer and gave me a lopsided grin. I drove through thunderstorms, dust, up and down hills shaped like the word Alabama, through fleets and convoys of gnats and mosquitoes that coated the windshield like rain. I prefer the soul's means of transportation, which is strictly musical.

When I arrived in Louisiana, I didn't know where I was. I did have my piano with the depressed keys. It sat in the living room and waited for a blind tuner. What music I could get from it, I had to sneak out for myself. When I hit a note that wasn't there, I sang it instead.

The piano was put to my name at a time my mother thought she was dying. It was an unwanted legacy. She began to speak of her "will," a document that never got written. Her "will" was her way of talking about her death. It was funny she never left one, since her "will" in the other sense had been indelible. She had written that one all over my life.

"Come in the living room," she said one day, "I want to discuss the music." We moved slowly, she holding on to my arm. I helped her down the step to the living room where the piano had sat for years, unplayed. The music? I guessed she meant the piano again. I held the wooden chair steady as she sat down.

"What do you mean, the music?"

"I want the music to be dignified. Do you have any suggestions?"

I couldn't think of what to say. The music.

"No, Mom."

"Maybe you could ask the cantor. I'd like him to sing."

"This is hard to talk about."

"I don't want a funeral like Jack Bernstein's. That was so cold and impersonal. They didn't even pronounce his name right. I want someone who knows me. I want the cantor to sing."

She knew what she wanted. She wanted a song. "What is it," she said, "you know the one they always sing . . . *El Moley Rachamim* . . . da da da . . ." That was the music she wanted, rich and dignified. And for once, loud. She wanted a song with heart.

A few months later she was back in the hospital. Visiting was painful; she had stopped speaking. I sat by her bed for an hour, talking, wiping her face with a washcloth, swabbing her lips with lemon-glycerine sticks, trying to let her know I was there. But she said nothing. It was desperate and yet very quiet, late afternoon in the hospital between shifts, an overcast day.

"Am I upside down?" she asked suddenly. A child's voice.

"No."

"I spoke to you last night, but you didn't answer."

"I wasn't here last night."

She cried. "Will you sing a song for me?"

I sang "Home on the Range," "God Bless America," "Celia." I sang "Loch Lomond" and "Comin' Through the Rye." "If a body meet a body / comin' through the rye. / If a body kiss a body . . ."

All my life, I'd felt my mother's sadness as a song without lyrics. The sadness was all that her secrecy would allow; the lyrics—the actual facts, were denied us. We didn't know exactly who she was.

She could not hide her past completely. There were facts. There were persons. But there was no way to fit them into any pattern. They appeared strangely, and without explanation. One of them was a woman I knew as Agnes.

4

cracked eggs

I was fifteen years old. My mother took me along, as witness or buffer. The last thing I wanted was to be in the Church Home Hospital where Agnes, a woman I hardly knew, lay dying. The poor woman moaned and sweated while my mother and Aunt Rachel, her sister, perched on either side of her bed like the donors of a triptych. The central tableau was dominated by the swell of her stomach, an imitation of pregnancy that made me sick. I had a teenager's intolerance for physical defects. A mop of white scraggly hair formed a corona about her round, nearly featureless face. I felt pity for her, but I had spent no more than a few hours with Agnes in my entire life, and those under false pretenses.

My mother asked her how she was feeling and Agnes moaned. Aunt Rachel stuck an ice cube in her mouth. The two sisters had little to say to each other. I thumbed through magazines. The doctors in this down-at-the-heels hospital were all foreign born. Agnes's doctor was Korean, and I remember his answer when my mother collared him in the hallway. "How is she doing?" The doctor blinked through black frames. "She is yes-no getting better." I have never been able to untorture that syntax but have often thought since that it had a certain ludicrous wisdom and might serve as a universal prognosis.

When I was eight I used to dread a certain trip I would take on a Sunday with my mother. "Come on," she would say, "we are going on a picnic." I didn't want to go. But my mother would give me one of her looks. Her face would be tight and her voice had a metallic edge. I knew if I objected she would blow up. All the more I didn't want to go. But I had to.

She brought hard-boiled eggs, carefully wrapped in plastic bags, two for each of us. I would sit in the front seat of the Chevrolet and stare out the window, angry. "We're going to have a picnic," my mother would say.

She was apprehensive. I felt it in her voice. She wasn't fooling me with talk of a picnic. Hard-boiled eggs, white lumps.

We travelled Liberty Road, a two-lane highway that petered out into a country lane. General stores with white peeling paint, pocked and rusted Pepsi signs, dusty bags of feed. Between gas stations: miles of fences and fields. "Look at the cows," my mother said. I looked. "Where are we going?" The wheels rolled, the sunshine vivid and bright.

At last Liberty Road gave out and we veered west, winding and twisting through slight hills. I beat my hand against the window, singing to myself, my mother silent and preoccupied. I imagined my fingers ended in a magic sword blade that stretched malevolently to the horizon. I could cut trees off at the trunk and houses, cars, and people. We were going to see Agnes.

We went through the gates and up a gravel driveway. A brick institutional building, squat and official, sat on a small rise. It seemed surprising and ugly in this landscape where everything else was barn, farm house or country store. Walking slowly, the nurses brought Agnes, a round woman in a faded blue gingham dress. We took her with us in the car. I sat in the back.

When we had driven far enough away that the hospital was no longer in sight, we got out of the car and my mother and I spread a red blanket on the grass while Agnes stood uncertainly watching us. She said nothing. She smelled of lavender and had too much powder on her face. Her lipstick was an alarming shade of bright red and floated far above her lips, like a clown's makeup, giving her smile a fuzzy off-centered lift, as though a bird had taken flight. Her eyes were blue and did not focus.

My mother took out the eggs and, to amuse me, we made a contest of cracking shells. She moistened a handkerchief with her tongue and rubbed the stray lipstick off Agnes's lip. The whole time, she was talking to her:

"How are you feeling?"

"Fine."

"Are you eating well?"

"Yes."

"Isn't it a pretty day? The sun is shining."

"Yes."

The drive back was always silent.

In arguments, I would sometimes blurt out, "You're crazy." Then my mother would glare at me in fury and between her teeth would say, "Don't ever call me that. I'm not crazy." Her insistence went beyond the context of the argument and she would repeat it, breaking into tears that frightened me, "Don't ever call me crazy."

In 1965, when I was fifteen, Rachel decided to pull Agnes out of the state hospital after thirty years and care for her at home. Soon my mother agreed to alternate with her. This cooperative arrangement did not last very long. Agnes took sick almost immediately and within a few months the two sisters were together—for the last time— watching her die of stomach cancer in the Church Home

30

Hospital. The same hospital where, years later, my mother also died.

I do remember Agnes's brief stay with us. My sisters were away at college, and she slept in their room. For her first meal, Agnes sat at the table, smelling of lavender, silently mashing her peas and potatoes with a fork. The fork moved up and down while I stared, then looked away, so as not to bother my mother, whose grief was evident. There was something so lost about Agnes, so abandoned and weightless, as if she might float up out of the chair if we didn't hold her down.

That same night I woke around midnight. I heard water running in the bathroom. My eyes burned in the harsh light. Agnes was on her hands and knees. Beside her were two cans of Ajax and a box of lavender powder. She was dipping a red towel into the toilet bowl, sprinkling it with lavender and Ajax, and scrubbing the tile. The mixture left thick blue swirls. She had already done the mirror, the bathtub, the sink basin, the metal fixtures, and the walls.

"I'm cleaning," she volunteered as I stood there, watching. I had no idea what to say. I felt pity, and, strangely, hatred. I hated her for existing, since she hadn't existed up until then. My mother appeared behind me, bent down, and lifted Agnes by the arms. "Ma," she said softly, "it's too late."

I remember that as the first time I really understood that Agnes was her mother. I suppose we children knew who she was, but the fact was never referred to. We never called her Grandmother. Neither did my mother ever explain how Agnes had ended up at the state mental hospital.

Why had my mother hidden her past? She denied her mother and father, and for years at a time she did not see her sister, even though we all lived in the same city.

But in the year of mourning her sister Rachel came back. At my mother's grave, she wept and spoke terrible words.

31

5

on mourning

My mother was buried by the Sol Levinson Brothers. They have a monopoly on Jewish funerals in Baltimore, conducting two a day. Immediately to the north side of the chapel, a long hallway leads to an anteroom. My family came there by way of an underground passage, avoiding the long line of mourners snaking through the hall above us. We could hear them though, chattering. My chest tightened at the sound of their voices.

In the chapel, one of the assistants came to perform the ceremony of rending. He was programmatically solemn and wore a cheap dark suit with gapped shirt buttons. He pinned a black ribbon to my lapel, took out a Gem razor blade, and sliced it. A two thousand year old custom.

The Talmud is very specific about the rules for rending clothes. It is very specific about every conceivable subject. Its great virtue as a book of wisdom lies in its nagging detail. The Talmud has been described as the book most resembling the sea. It is the continuous record of debate and *pilpul* over a thousand years, from the time of the first rabbis to the middle ages. Conceptually it is a labyrinth; in print it resembles a maze, a small shrub of law surrounded by hedges of commentary, and these further bordered by footnotes. The distance from the center to the outer path is 1300 years.

The tractate on mourning is greatly concerned with rending. A Jew must tear his clothes immediately upon learning of the death of a close relative. This gesture, so clear and direct, is then nearly obscured in quibbles. The rabbis imagine darkly. They ask, if a man has ten sons and all die at once, does he rend ten times? (No, only once.) A man learns his mother has died and rends his garment. Later, he finds the news was garbled; his father has died. Should he tear again? (No.) A man rends for his cousin then learns it is his mother . . .

Who knows just how far to rend? The rabbis disagree. "How far does one rend? As far as his navel. According to others, as far as the breast."

I did not rend to the navel. I did not rend according to the Talmud. I did not rend at all. I did not take my shirt the moment I saw my mother die and rip it down to my breast. I did not tear the suit I wore the day of her funeral even though it was one she had bought me, did not tear it down the sleeves to leave my arms bare, as used to be the custom so anciently even the first rabbis couldn't explain it. I did not go barefoot to the cemetery. I did not rend, I did not rip, I did not tear. And so, though the Talmud speaks of basting the torn garments when mourning is done, I did not baste, I have not basted.

My daughter Anya was born the year my mother died. I remember her head being turned, the rest of her still in her mother's body. Her hair was kinked and matted with blood. Mother and daughter were connected by a blue cord, so beautifully twined, resilient, strong.

I watched the doctor sew Moira up, for the baby's head was large and had torn my wife's body. He sewed with long strokes, raising his hand high, like my grandfather the tailor busy at his work. He might have been whistling as he basted.

And so I might answer the rabbis: I should have torn as far as the navel since that is the visible sign of my birth and first separation. As the umbilical cord was cut, so should the last cord between mother and son have been honored. Between breast and navel, no contradiction. For as the prophet Joel writes, "Rend your heart and not your garments."

In the chapel anteroom, the day my mother was buried, the ribbon pinned to my suit seemed removed, the symbol of a symbol. The undertaker's assistant repeated a prayer in chopped up Hebrew, one syllable at a time. The tatters of a prayer.

At that moment, Aunt Rachel walked in. I hadn't seen my mother's sister in fifteen years.

"Do you talk to her any more?" I'd asked my mother.

"We write." My mother grinned like a fox.

"What do you say to each other?"

My mother gave me an envelope. Inside, a Hallmark greeting card. On the bottom, "your sister Rachel." That was what fifty years had come to.

I remember Aunt Rachel vividly from childhood. She was exotic to me then because she smoked cigarettes and drank wine in the afternoon. She sat in a large overstuffed green chair with her legs crossed at the knee. She was wearing dark hose. Cigarette in one hand, smoke drifting around her head, she had my mother's nose but somewhat larger, like a beak.

She'd lived in Italy after the war and so represented to me the glamor of travel. She had once given me a globe, that is, the world. The world was round and turquoise and there were apparently other places beyond the safety of Forest Hill Road with its neat brick tract homes, trim lawns and fences. She had given me sepia postcards of person-ages and ruined buildings in Italy. Sepia seemed to me for-ever an exotic and somehow sexy color. Aunt Rachel in sepia: the photo tinted with the coffee she always drank and the brown stains on her teeth from cigarettes, and even the wine, dark red, darkened into sepia-black and her lipstick, nail polish, stockings, all sepia. She gave me a small green book with blank pages in which, as a teenager, I wrote my first poems.

When she entered the chapel, no one knew what to do, though it couldn't have been so surprising. I touched Rachel's hand, gave her a black ribbon—promptly ripped—and asked her to ride with us to the cemetery. In the car, I felt the strain. She resembled my mother entirely, which made the trip eerie. She had my mother's knack for inspir-ing discomfort.

My mother was buried in the spring, and it wasn't until the Jewish New Year that I saw Rachel again. Because of the dream in which my mother told me that the dead wait for Kaddish prayers, I decided to observe the High Holidays in a certain worn and decrepit shul in East Baltimore. It was the last relic of the great Jewish immigrant community from the early part of the century. It was also the shul of my mother's father, my grandfather Benjamin.

The old ghetto was no more. The stores, homes, shuls, the old Yiddish theater, were all abandoned. Physically, the House of Israel was falling apart, paint peeling, pews cracked and scarred. Once I even saw a cockroach crawling up the skirt of the Holy Torah. The Holy Ark had a faded purple velveteen curtain; its pull rope was a worn gold braid that needed hard jerking, and often the curtain came off its runners.

The congregants were a mixed batch, poor and old for the most part. Jews in work shirts, one with AMOCO stitched on his pocket. An old man who wore two pairs of glasses, one over the other. He had a long white beard and looked like a child's idea of God. He fell asleep during the service. Another regular came that Rosh Hashonah with a bandage over his eye. A man davening next to him, in yarmulke, tallis and Hawaiian shirt, tried to adjust the old man's eyepatch, addressing whomever would listen, "What can I do? He won't let me help him."

The young rabbi was in his early forties, husky, with a dark black beard. He prayed enthusiastically, chanting in a rich baritone. He was a steelworker. Every so often, he would jerk his head violently and shout BEH! Then he would go back to his prayer calmly. The poor man, we learned in loud whispers around the congregation, had been injured at work. A beam had fallen on his head. This mundane explanation did no justice to the mysterious and otherworldly BEH! which had angelic or demonic undertones. Either way, BEH! pointed to a superior force utterly possessing his body and so gave his prayers a poignancy they might otherwise have lacked. When he chanted with his twelve-year-old son, their voices blended into honey.

Mr. Feiman, who functioned as *shammash*, gave the New Year sermon. He stood on the pulpit, a short man in droopy faded clothes with hound dog folds in his cheeks, and gave an impassioned incomprehensible plea, slipping back and forth between English and Yiddish.

"This is the *alte shul* in *Oste* Baltimore . . ." Tears streamed down his cheeks as he got carried away with himself, trying to raise money to paint the walls. He owned a clothing store a block away. The ghetto had changed from Jewish to black, and there were few customers for his ancient merchandise. In his store window was a large sign, lettered L-O-O-K, with two eyes painted in the O's, and an arrow that pointed to a wonder: a mammoth pair of pants with three legs.

There were many delights in that shul. Too poor to buy

fancy new prayer books, they made do with the most po-
etic liturgy I had ever read, wonderful kabbalistic texts
from the last century. The prayers mentioned ranks of angels I had never heard of, like the ophanim, who float
somewhere beyond the cherubim and seraphim. There
were also literal and fervid descriptions of God's holy throne
and of atmospheric and melodic conditions in the world
to come.

While the old-timers davened in rapid-fire Hebrew, I
thumbed through the prayer book, reading the graphic
tales of martyrs, how Rabbi Akiba, for instance, refused to
remove his tefillin from his forehead and wrist, and so the
Romans stripped his skin in a spiral like an apple peel,
and still he went on saying Shema: Hear O Israel, the Lord
our God, the Lord is One.

From some of the mystical poetry, I got at least a hint
of what Judaism must be like for fervent believers. However compromised and skeptical I might be, I was not im-
mune to a sensation of pure Judaism. If a religion can be
reduced to a sensation, then Judaism was a crystalline,
needle-like whiteness. Perhaps it was the white north light
bathing the old synagogue. But I felt the unity the Shema
speaks of. With it came a sense of peace.

Granted the shul was vulgar and noisy. Those who associate religion with decorum could not experience what I
experienced there. The House of Israel was too poor to be
anything but real. When the customary New Year pledges
were requested, I promised twenty-five dollars and for
that sum I was called up by Mr. Feiman for an "honor" at
the altar.

I said the blessing for reading from the Torah and then
hunched over the scroll as the rabbi read from it, pointing
at each word with a silver finger, the yod. When he finished,
the chazzan whispered, asking if I wanted a special prayer.
I requested one in my mother's honor.

I was hoping to make amends for my neglect. All that spring and summer, I had failed to say Kaddish, as a good son ought. I didn't believe in organized religions and after a year of watching my mother die, I was in no mood for going through the motions. Yet I knew that for many Jews the culmination of earthly happiness was to raise a son who would say Kaddish. Even my mother, otherwise non-observant, had paid an orphan at the Ner Israel Rabbinical Academy to say Kaddish for her father.

I knew it was a beautiful prayer. It had served the earliest Jewish mystics as a mantra, transporting them in a trance to God's throne. There the mystic would join angels repeating the prayer in constant praise of God's name. I knew it was a prayer of praise, a mourner's prayer that never mentions death.

Sometimes, I had worried that there was such a thing as the spirit and that my mother was suffering somewhere in Jewish limbo for lack of Kaddish prayer from her son. After I dreamed about it, I did pull a prayer book from the shelf and mumble a Kaddish, even though I knew, properly, it needed to be said in a synagogue. But my religious sensibility is unorthodox. I figured God wouldn't mind, especially the sort of God I figured on, a God who was not stern, but easy-going like me.

I counted on my mother's ghost to forgive me, even forgive me for only half-believing in ghosts. After all, there is something that survives in us after someone dies. And that part does haunt us. We say in the Kaddish, "God is Great," not for the sake of our dead, but to impose a limit on their influence. God is great, we pray—and you are just dead.

As I left the synagogue of my grandfather, I saw my mother in the vestibule. She was sitting at a bench with a large prayer book opened in front of her. She did not appear to be reading it, just staring as I had stared while the others prayed.

I was shocked until I saw who she was, the only person she could be, Aunt Rachel.

I asked her how she was doing. She immediately asked me if I had been to the cemetery. No, I had neglected that as well; I was a terrible mourner. She told me about a custom during the Days of Awe, that is, the days between Rosh Hashonah and The Day of Atonement. It is a special time to visit the dead.

That made sense to me. The High Holy Days were the period of reconciliation. Before a Jew can ask for forgiveness from God he must make peace with his family and friends. With the dead as well as the living.

Moira and I went to the cemetery that afternoon. There was a slight breeze as we walked past the gatehouse. We moved slowly down the hill to my mother's grave. The ground was still raw.

I closed my eyes and tried to imagine my mother was with us under our feet. In that heap of dirt. I tried to imagine her physically, her bones, the skin wearing off her face. Amazingly, I felt her presence. It was the sensation of someone entering a room when your back is turned. Moira felt it too, as a hard contraction, hard enough to make her falter. She held my hand to steady herself. In the car, the contractions were coming so fast we didn't try to time them. We raced to the hospital.

As my daughter was born, I kept thinking of my mother's presence in the cemetery. And I remembered my mother's words in the dream. For hadn't the birth of my daughter and the visit to the cemetery come together in a single wave, mixed in a pattern too complex to describe easily, but palpable as a splash of water all the same?

I did not see Aunt Rachel again until the unveiling. A year had passed since my mother's funeral and our family gathered together at the cemetery to officially dedicate her tombstone. It was a bright spring day. Anya Miriam, at six

39

months, was in her stroller, wearing a white bonnet. I had given her my mother's name, Miriam, as part of her own.

When the brief ceremony began, I saw Aunt Rachel coming slowly toward us down the hill. She stood apart from us. She had buried her father, mother and sister, and now she was alone.

My father asked Aunt Rachel to join us at the house for a meal. I was assigned to bring her. But as we started to leave, Aunt Rachel fell to her knees and hugged my mother's stone. Tears streamed down her face. "Leave me here, I want to stay with my sister."

I was furious. Worst of all, she reminded me of my mother. The same tacky melodrama *she* was capable of if it meant getting her way. I hardened my heart and said softly in her ear, "Okay, we'll see you later." I wouldn't give her the satisfaction of making a scene.

Aunt Rachel sobbed, looking into my mother's tombstone as though she were reading a text there. "*You* were never there when I needed you." Was she talking to me—or to my mother?

The week my mother died, Rachel had visited her in the hospice. She had walked into her room, had stood at the foot of her bed. My mother was weak and hadn't been talking to anyone. We thought she was asleep. But Miriam lifted her head from the pillow and fixed her eyes on Rachel. She didn't want pity. She said, "Why did you come—now?"

You were never there when I needed you. Why did you come—now? I hear the words resonate, but the voices change. At times, my mother could have made those accusations against me. At times, I might have made them against her.

You were never there when I needed you. Spoken by me, the words were true in this sense: my mother had never told me properly who "she" was.

6

on typology

My mother tried an interesting experiment with her children. She erased her past. Throughout my childhood, she pretended that her parents never existed, that she herself never existed until she became our mother.

She did not say, I have a father, I have a mother, but I would rather not talk about it. She was silent. And over the years she was silent about her silence.

This lasted into our adulthood. My sister once told her future in-laws that her grandparents were dead. A few weeks later, she had to cancel an engagement party because her dead grandfather died.

I sometimes wondered if my mother believed that in telling the story, her life would end. She adopted a strategy of silence, erased herself, and then wrote Miriam Kamenetz on a blank sheet of paper.

It seems amazing to me that my mother so restrained our natural curiosity, or that, after a time, we so restrained ourselves. Not to ask my mother about her past was to be "polite" and good. We grew up in the silence of her secret. This was the sad music I felt near my mother, the music she wished me to play on the piano. I came to love secrecy myself. Without realizing it, I repeated the pattern, a typology that frustrated her.

"Why won't you tell me what you're thinking?" she would challenge me. "You never tell me where you are going," she'd say ruefully. And plaintively, "Is there anything you want to tell your mother?"

"Nothing," I'd say, annoyed.

A child cannot be without a history. Yet sometimes I think there is another extreme, to know too much. To recognize that one's life is not original, that one is merely reenacting a typology, some Grandfather Benjamin's life, some Uncle Abraham's.

A medieval scholastic quibble has it that there is no free will. For an action has a cause, that cause has a cause and so on back through time. So it is impossible that anyone should act out of free will.

The argument is, in a sense, unanswerable, except that it takes a retrospective point of view. It is regressive, not predictive. Having acted, I may deduce the cause, but from the act, I cannot predict the effect.

Perhaps we have lost the ability of prophecy because we are so used to reading books. A Gypsy told me once that she would never let her children go to school to learn to read.

"Why?"

"Because then they won't be able to read tea leaves."

Yet a Jew cannot believe in tea leaves, for he feels his future is written in one torah or another. When we shape a story, we shape it to our own ends—and out of our own beginnings. Every mind structures its world into a family. The great founding act of any science—Mendeleev's in chemistry, Linnaeus' in biology—is creating a family from formerly unrelated elements. Linnaeus' charts and Mendeleev's periodic table are family trees.

The Jewish metaphor for this is a book, a Torah. The legend has it that Moses gave the Torah to all the Jewish people, those living, and those yet to be born. Each Jewish soul guards one letter from that day. Which means: the body of Israel is altogether the body of a book.

Do we read the book, or does the book read us? Haunted by the story, do we project it back into history? Do we re-create our personal lives according to remembered patterns, shaping an inevitability that might otherwise not be there?

I have before me not a Torah, but a simple family history. They are not the same, though the Torah is, in a sense, a family history. In Paris, a rabbi told me the story of his friend, a Yugoslavian Marxist. In his youth the man had been a Catholic seminarian. But one day he looked up from his Bible and said, "What does this have to do with me—Abraham? Jacob? David?—this family history of a tiny tribe in Israel? I'm a Croat!"

There are Jews, too, who want to escape typology. They find history too stultifying. In the Passover Haggadah, the story is told of four sons: the wise, the wicked, the simple, and the silent. The wicked son asks, "What mean *ye* by this service?" And the father is instructed to "set his teeth on edge," "By saying *ye* and not *we* you exclude yourself from the people of Israel. Had *ye* been there, *ye* would not have been delivered with us." Even the wicked son cannot escape easily. His story is told in the book.

For Jews, a letter of the story is planted in each child's name. Rodger Lee Kamenetz is my secular name. But as a Jew I have a secret name. I am "Rafol," Rafael, or "healed-by-God." A medical angel. Such names are given as a memorial to a dead relative. As Rafol I am the heir of "Frank" Caplan. In Hebrew we are both Rafols. And though I see no physical resemblance between this elderly smiling gentleman with the white handlebar moustaches and myself, we are equally *rafol* (healed) in my mother's affection.

43

Healed and annealed, joined by a magic of naming, a typology whose force is inescapable and whose name is love.

Yet Jewish lives have been shaped tragically by an overwhelming historical typology. The Kabbalah conceives that each man, in his individual history, relives the great moments of biblical history: the deliverance from Egypt, the wandering in the desert. The story of exile repeats itself in Jewish life again and again. The very word Hebrew seems to mean "one from the other side of the river," a stranger, a wanderer. The story of my grandfather Benjamin and of thousands of other Jewish immigrants is prefigured. A painful displacement ruined his life and crushed the spirit of thousands of others. It is a type of the story of Jacob and Laban. The Jew lives among strangers, as Jacob lived at the whim of Laban, as my ancestors lived in Lithuania and the Ukraine.

I felt that I had been privileged to be raised apart from this. My mother, by separating us from her past, had helped to insulate me from the sad general history. Only her fear of death released her from her fear of telling us her life. One night, she gave her children their poor torah at last.

She was certain the next morning she would die in surgery. So she was able to tell my brother and me the whole story. We were sitting quietly in her hospital room on orange plastic chairs. She was propped up in bed with pillows. We stayed long past visiting hours that night. After a time the nurses stopped checking in on us, the hospital grew very quiet, and so sweet was the effect, I wished her story would not end.

Agnes Caplan Kierr Van Meter. As my mother told it, what a tragic writing of names my grandmother had. She was born in St. Louis, Missouri, around 1900. Her father, Rafol "Frank" Caplan, had come, like many Latvian Jews, to St. Louis to be in the brewery business.

Agnes's mother, Etta, died in childbirth. Frank and his infant daughter went to Baltimore where Agnes was brought up by Frank's widowed sister, Riva Sodden. Tanta Riva was *"fromm,"* that is, sternly religious. "Even the most Orthodox considered her too Orthodox," my mother said.

Frank Caplan's sister Lena (who gave me my middle name, Lee) was married to Julius Kierr, a wealthy lawyer and merchant in Ponnevez, in Lithuania.

Ponnevez was an important Jewish ghetto, with established institutions of Jewish learning and many fine synagogues. Julius Kierr was a wealthy merchant and lawyer. But at the end of the nineteenth century, conditions grew difficult for Jews and all but three of his children emigrated to America.

Benjamin Kierr, like his Biblical namesake, was the youngest son. Studious, moody, his mother's favorite, as a boy he wanted to become a rabbi. Benjamin studied Talmud at an early age. Had he remained in Europe, he might have pursued his studies and died with his aunts in the concentration camps. But he followed his older sisters to America, expecting them to put him through law school. He was shocked when they told him to find work.

Benjamin Kierr was learned in the Talmud, but he had no skills to speak of. He began to sell barbershop equipment—scissors, combs, chairs—work he assured himself was temporary until he could find a job worthy of his intelligence. On Shabbas, he spent the day in shul, praying, studying the beloved intricacies of the law.

Eventually, Benjamin became a barber. He would start a shop, build up the business, and sell it at a profit, moving on to a new shop. Perhaps the restlessness of the man showed here. Or did he think that each time he sold, he was finished with the hated barbering business forever and ready to start a serious career?

At one point, Benjamin Kierr had a shop on Lombard Street in the heart of the old East Baltimore Jewish ghetto.

Around the corner was The House of Israel, the synagogue where Aunt Rachel and I prayed the year my mother died. His spirit attracted us there.

He used to sit in the downstairs study, reading from ancient volumes of the Talmud published in Lithuania. They are still there, yellowed pages, cracked bindings. He discussed the law on Saturday mornings, munching on kichel (sugar cakes) and sipping schnapps, for after the morning prayers there would be a little Oneg Shabbat (rejoicing in the sabbath). It was a world where he could forget his frustrations.

Agnes Caplan was already engaged to another man when she met her first cousin, Benjamin Kierr. She was "swept off her feet" as my mother put it. Even then, so many years later it could not matter, all of them dead, my mother dying, there was a rueful tone in her voice, as though just at that point in the story she had isolated the nub of disaster. The tone seemed to say, if only here I could stop the story, then everything might have been different.

How did they appear at that time? Benjamin was strong looking, broad but not stout, with dark wavy hair and a brushy moustache. The eyes were extraordinarily firm, full of self-assurance, perhaps cruel. Agnes had short straight hair, flipped up around her ears, a round face, very soft in its effects and eyes that seemed always to gaze beyond. The eyes gave her a half-dissociated look.

Of course, such a reading of their photographs is specious. It is the old fallacy again, reading the future back into the past. Benjamin's cruelty, Agnes's madness—how could I help but find them in their features?

Frank Caplan disliked his nephew and opposed the marriage. But his daughter wouldn't listen. He even warned Agnes that this *fromm* barber would beat her. "He might hit me once," Agnes told him, "but he wouldn't do it again."

Immigrant Jews rarely married for romance. Her father's

opposition must have added spice to the most ordinary event in the world, a Jew marrying her cousin. A marriage that meant what? A return to the blood, an enfolding. For though Agnes rebelled by opposing her father's wishes, she rebelled merely to return. Tanta Riva, who had raised her with many a beating, was re-embodied in Benjamin. Did Agnes conceive as romance ("swept off her feet") what was merely a spark of recognition? She soon learned her mistake. Benjamin beat Agnes often, and in front of the children.

Jewish law, in the hands of a cruel person, could provide many excuses for a beating. There were so many things a wife could do wrong, so many punctilios of the law. The separate dishes for milk and meat. The rules regarding the Sabbath, intercourse, cleanliness. And Benjamin, who had failed to find a place for himself in the new world, no doubt clung all the more fiercely to the rules of the old one.

Finally, Agnes left. She ran off with the proverbial traveling salesman, a "drummer." My mother was ten.

The stories about Agnes after this are fuzzy. One version is that the "drummer" beat her as well, perhaps so severely as to damage her brain.

Eventually Agnes returned to Baltimore. She married a Dutch longshoreman named Van Meter. I don't know how many years elapsed. I can imagine Benjamin Kierr though, embarrassed, embittered and guilty: his wife not only shames him by running away but returns to Baltimore and marries a Gentile.

Agnes's second husband was an alcoholic, my mother said, but she loved him very much. When he died, she began to wander the streets near the waterfront in a daze. Benjamin, hearing of it, took steps to have her placed in a state mental institution. The last thirty years of her life until the year she died were spent as a patient at Springfield State Hospital.

Grandfather Benjamin never visited our house though he lived about two miles from us. He always found an excuse not to come. Once we did visit him. I recall an old dark house with stuffed chairs, an old man sitting stiffly in one of them.

Mainly, he left me the memory of his funeral, a strangely empty memory of shoveling snow early one morning. I was to get the job done quickly because, my mother said, "your grandfather died." Later that morning Aunt Rachel came over, along with other relatives I didn't know, stepping along the path I'd cleared. I was struck, at ten years old, with the rather abstract thought that "death has entered my life." It was ironic enough. The news of his death was the first time I'd given the man any thought at all.

When Agnes left the house, Miriam was ten, Rachel a teenager. Benjamin felt he could not raise his daughters. He sent them out to live with relatives. For a time, Miriam lived with her grandfather, Frank, my Hebrew namesake. There is a photograph of her, a young woman hugging the shoulder of a seated dapper man with white moustaches and kind eyes. She loved him very much. But Miriam's stay was only temporary.

I know more about my grandparents' lives than I know about my mother's. I don't know what it was like for her to be a child. What it felt like to see her mother beaten, what was said in the room the night that Agnes ran away. I know she did not come out of this with any great love of the Jewish religion. It was burned out of her, seared by hatefulness. I know she was afraid of becoming insane and felt primitively that it might be contagious.

At the same time, she admired Agnes. "She was ahead of her time," my mother said, wistfully. For a woman to have a sense of self, a sense of a life on her own, no matter how thwarted, or confused . . .

That is the precious thing my mother brought out of her

childhood. A life so sad, she left it blank. I never heard from her a single incident—no anecdote of her father, no image of her mother. I don't know what her house looked like, what toys she played with. It was as though she had never been a child. It was all wiped out, all burned at the edges. She did tell me that, when she was nine, the Kierr family went back to Lithuania and visited the old aunts and uncles. I'd seen her passport. But when I asked her about it, eager to know more, all she would tell me was, "Every one of them died in the holocaust."

Even though both her mother and her father abandoned her, she did not abandon herself. One night her father must have said to her, in words something like this, "I am sorry, but I cannot keep you. You'll have to live with your grandfather." Then her grandfather could not keep her, and her aunt could take only one child and chose Rachel. So my mother, as a teenager, came to live with a foster family. Even after Benjamin remarried, he never took her back.

Out of this came a fierce drive. It was all mind over matter, will over circumstance. There was nothing she couldn't do or be if she determined it. Yet she had nothing, no money, no mother, no prospects. She had to drop out of school at age sixteen. She was always ashamed of that.

She took a job in a Woolworth's. She sold perfume and cheap jewelry. And then, one summer, when she was eighteen, she hitchhiked with Rachel to Atlantic City. They slept under the boardwalk until they got jobs working as chambermaids in a hotel.

Atlantic City was a popular vacation spot for East Coast Jews. There Rachel met Louis Kamenetz, but he was soon attracted to her younger sister, Miriam. Rachel was intelligent but austere. Miriam was clever, talkative and liked to have a good time.

My father's brother Louis was a year and a half older. But Irvin was his mother's favorite. He skipped a grade in school and so outshined his brother that Louis dropped out to avoid the embarrassment. So the rival sisters met a pair of rival brothers.

The older brother meets the older sister, but rejects her for the younger sister. Then the younger sister meets the younger brother and rejects the older brother for him. It is a pretty dance, a minuet of rejection.

And was the dance necessary to the romance? Had my father not met my mother in just this way, if they had met on their own, would they have fallen in love?

The story fits a typology. For eventually my father's brother left Baltimore and settled in Newark. One thinks of Cain and Abel, Isaac and Ishmael, Jacob and Esau, warring brothers. Jacob, the younger, who through his mother's love, wins the birthright due his older brother. And Esau exiled to New Jersey.

Typology hangs over each Jew, as oracle and threat. And romantic love, which for Jews is really a very alien cultural invention—having sprung from the troubadour culture—confuses the issue. What we call love is perhaps often the same emotion one feels from a satisfying story. Love is a plot that clicks into place, that resonates with a story already told. Agnes fell in love with Benjamin; he "swept her off her feet" my mother told me, weeping years later. Was it love, or was it recognition—you are the missing character in a story my genes wish to repeat?

What makes us attracted in spite of ourselves, in spite of our parents' pleadings? To fall in love, to be swept off your feet, is to become a character in a story. Events move you along, free will takes a holiday, and there is the delicious sense of escape. The irony is that you are not freeing yourself, but losing your freedom to the story.

The saving grace is our ignorance. We do not know whose history we are enacting. We do not see the repetitions standing behind the act. My mother "cuts off" her neighbor, Mrs. Abrams, for some imagined slight. She strikes her off her list. She does not see that behind this rejection, is her father rejecting her, and behind that is her grandfather Frank leaving Agnes with Tanta Riva, and behind that who knows what series of rejections and denials.

My parents married in the flurry of weddings that took place at the beginning of World War II. They lived together at a training camp in South Carolina until my father was shipped overseas to England.

My mother moved in with her in-laws. It could not have been a comfortable three years. Grandmother Kamenetz was suspicious of her and had opposed the marriage. She considered her son, who after all, had been "college educated," as too good for Miriam. Grandpa Kamenetz was also suspicious. He objected to my father's leaving my mother his car. He removed the wheels and put the car up on blocks. "And he was right," my mother told us, laughing, "even though it made me mad at the time."

When my father returned from the war, he came back to two-year-old twin daughters he had never seen and a wife he had known for less than a year. Some of his pharmacist friends were using the GI Bill to go back to school and become doctors. My father had a job at Read's Drugstore and was making twenty-five dollars a week. My mother and his mother united in urging him to return to school, but he felt he was too far behind already.

My father always regretted that decision. And he passed that regret on to me. "I could have been a doctor," he would sigh after an especially rough day at the store. "He could have been a doctor," my mother would say, after paying a visit to Dr. Bernstein. "I told him he should have been a doctor," my grandfather echoed. "A doctor holds out his hand and says, 'Five dollars please. Thank you. Next. Five

51

dollars please, thank you.'" And my grandfather would chuckle, his palm stretched out in front of him, the "easy five" laying in his hand.

When I was a child, I never had any idea of what I wanted to be. So powerful was the radiation of my father's regret that it obliterated the idea of any career. I didn't want to work. I remember filling out a Merit Scholarship survey after graduating from college. The surveyors wished to know which profession I intended to pursue, now that the business corporations of America had so generously staked me to a Yale education. I scribbled, "Housewife."

In thinking about these typologies, these pathetic retracings, I look at my own life in disgust. How could I have been such a puppet of repetition? How could I have been such a little character trapped in old patterns?

Then the sheer force of my mother's will comes home to me. I see that at a crucial point in her own life, perhaps as she met my father, my mother decided that there was no use to her history, no use to it at all. She erased her past and created something new. And in doing so, she thought to escape the cruel typology of Benjamin, the mad typology of Agnes.

But in the same gesture she broke the thread of her own story. She had no real grip on herself, no typology to help her understand her own angers. She never saw how she was like the father she had erased from her heart. The will power we so admired was also frightening. It could create, or destroy.

7

interior decoration

As I said, my mother never wrote a will. But her will was written all over my life, from the very beginning. I was a quiet boy. Often I was tongue-tied. The obvious questions took on amazing complications, and I was unable to follow simple directions. Adults made me uncomfortable. At five or six, I would go to knock at my friend's door and hesitate, afraid I'd make a grownup angry. I hoped someone would simply sense my presence. I was always afraid of disturbing things.

At night I'd wake and walk slowly down the hall. I'd pause and listen for a sound, calling, "Mom . . . Mom?" but my parents pretended not to hear. What was I afraid of?

There was a pressure inside me and a sadness. At night I had troubled sleep. Or I had the classic anxiety dream of falling. I was afraid if I landed, I would die. Often I would wake from such a dream, tangled in the sheets, my head on the floor.

I dreamed of falling well into my twenties. One night, as I approached the ground, I let myself fall. It was lucid dreaming. The closer I came, the softer the ground seemed. When I landed, the ground was warm and yielding flesh.

So that was the secret! I'd had no reason to be afraid. The field of my vision turned ninety degrees. I raced through a tunnel. I was not I, but a point of light. I was approaching a throbbing sphere, bulging with soft dark threads. With great pleasure, I knew the egg of my own conception.

All those years of childhood, I had been falling into the lap of my mother. My guilt was over her love. It was too strong for me. It was somehow inappropriate.

I couldn't reconcile my father's relative indifference with my mother's lavish praise. If I was nothing to him, I was everything to her: had I secretly won the Oedipal contest, taken my father's place in her heart? I didn't know that she had made me a substitute for the father who had rejected her, that she had named me after the grandfather she loved, and raised me to be father, grandfather, son and lover—her "sunshine boy."

I felt like screaming "No" and "no, no" in hot black sobs, but I said "Yes, I love you" in a cold strangled voice, birth of all future ambivalence. I would be lying in bed, tears on my cheeks, my mother stroking my hair, neck, back. How I hated her touch at those moments. I'd say any lie to get her away. This scene was repeated often in my childhood. My mother, after punishing me in anger, was begging my forgiveness while I was still furious.

Usually such scenes were precipitated by her cleaning frenzies. My mother had extremely ambivalent attitudes towards housework. For days she would neglect to sweep the floor, pick up newspapers or dust—and we children, sensing the relaxation, would follow suit, leaving beds unmade, socks flung on the floor. Then, without warning, or so it seemed to us, my mother would appear with a mop in one hand and an eerie gleam in her eye. Cleaning frenzy! Dust, papers, clothes, children would be swept before her. Her voice rose to shrieks: "*Shtonk*! Pick up your clothes!

54

God damn you!" Doors slammed, we scattered to our bedrooms. Each child cowered behind a door.

My mother's fury contrasted greatly with my father's calm demeanor. I don't remember his ever raising a hand to any of us, or his voice. If caught in one of my mother's storms, he was powerless to calm her. His placating tone usually made matters worse.

"What's the matter?" he would ask, blandly, innocently.

"What do you mean, can't you see what's the matter?" my mother would scream. "Everything's just fine with you. You work all day at the store. You don't know what's going on."

Cooking also made her angry. Many nights she would slam our plates in front of us, warning, "I'm aggravated" and we would sit on the edge of our seats, each hoping not to be the lightning rod, shoveling down our food and getting out. We all grew up skinny.

My mother made us crazy and yet we were crazy about her. We set our clocks to her moods. She was a spoiled powerful child, and we felt protective of her.

How I depended on her. If my mother were late coming home, I'd stare out the cold windowpane, my breath fogging it. I hoped to catch the first glimpse of her car. Then, in my anger, I'd punish her by imagining in great detail how she had died in a crash. I heard the policeman telling me, your mother died on Liberty Road. I saw the front door of the Chevrolet crushed, and I saw her handbag spilled open on the grass.

My mother had her secrets and I had mine. There was a pressure inside me, a pressure on words. I kept them from her as she had kept the story of her life from me.

I wanted to possess people completely. I loved exclusively. This was the love my mother had given me. "Who is the best mother in the whole world?" she would demand. As a toddler I must have given her complete devotion.

When I was older, I learned to withhold my love, to make a distance between us.

My mother made her own spaces. She stained her floors, papered her walls. Her redecorating channeled her violent desire for change. Every two years, she would completely redo the house. The decorator, an eternally enthusiastic young man with a dark purple wine stain on his temple, would unfurl the latest plans while my father pouted and grumbled. She hired an artist to cover a crack in the kitchen wall. He transformed it into an elegant blue tree with green leaves and purple peacocks.

In the sixties, she went Japanese. Shoji screens covered one whole wall of the living room although only a small window cowered behind them. To give the proper effect, fluorescent lights were installed, simulating daylight. The wall to wall was taken up, the floor sanded and stained a dark mahogany. As an eye-boggling centerpiece: the round orange rug.

I hated those floors. Every time we walked across them, our white footprints would show as dust. My mother would curse us, pushing a large buffing mop across our tracks. She demanded that we remove our shoes when we entered the house. The floor became the new flash point for her cleaning binges, and she damned the guilty party whose footprints remained as evidence.

My mother finally exhausted the decorative possibilities of our small brick tract home in the late sixties, the day she purchased black and white houndstooth wallpaper and covered every square inch of the kitchen including the ceiling. I lamented the loss of my peacock tree, and even my mother had to admit that the Op-art wallpaper was blinding.

She decided it was time to move. My father resisted. The house was paid for, he argued. He was getting older (fifty).

It didn't seem to be the time "to take on a new project" as he put it. But I had unwittingly provided my mother with a winning slogan, "Think rich."

She loved to repeat it, sometimes throwing it back in my face. I had just meant it as a way of telling her to loosen up, not worry so much about money. "Think rich, my son told me," she would say, mocking and laughing at the same time. Under the slogan "think rich" she launched her campaign for a new house. All of us were against it. I liked the old house, the old neighborhood where I had grown up. My father objected to the expense.

My parents' ideas about money had been shaped by the Depression. Even though my mother could be extravagant, it was a great sin, in her view, not to look for a bargain. She never bought *anything* that wasn't on sale.

Our family version of "I can get it for you wholesale" was "You can get *that* at the *store*," meaning my father's drugstore. But getting it at the store, when it didn't mean simply not getting it at all, usually implied a degradation of desire. A Monopoly set, gleaming in a department store window, became a yellowed Ben Hur Chariot game, dusty from months of sitting on the shelf.

I never wanted for anything essential. But I drew the conclusion that earning money, which occupied all of my father's time, and spending it, which occupied most of my mother's, were equally hard work. Where was the fun in it? What was the point? Why not think rich?

My mother's fitful cleaning rages, her periodic redecorations, her angry meals—these marked the patterns of my childhood. When she was sweet and easy with me, as often she was, I felt wonderful. No one was better than I was, she assured me, I was the best son in the world, brilliant, a genius, I could do anything I set my mind to. I was handsome too. And I believed her. I could bathe in her big warm cozy laughter. This intense mother love was addictive and unpredictable. How to turn it on, how to get it, how to stay on her good side, these were the questions around which my childhood revolved. With her approval I was everything. Without it, I was depressed, miserable, and desperate.

Then I rebelled. Puberty made me sarcastic and sullen. It also covered my face with red pimples, flags of revolution and hormonal desire. My mother launched a campaign to make me perfect again. The gap in my front teeth was attacked with rubber bands. I was trotted each week to the local dermatology mill. In a rat maze of plasterboard cubicles, hundreds of acne-coated teenagers awaited their fates. Plastic spoons were applied to our eyes, a dose of ultra-violet sunburned our skin. An hour after leaving, my face glowed Martian red, except for the white mark around my eyes. Instead of an unsightly teenager, I was a technicolor raccoon.

My nose gleamed with oil and sprouted red lanterns. Furiously I rubbed my blistered cheeks with sand-studded soap, pasted them with drying cream, but it was no use.

My mother took my face personally; my teeth, my hair, were all her responsibility. Looking at photographs, I see I was ugly: gap-toothed, raccoon-faced, pimply, with unruly curly hair combed up in a tumbling pompadour. My mother, grasping my chin in her hand, moved my head right and left. "How did I make such a beautiful child!"

When she said she made me, I think she meant it in every sense. I was her creation. Our lives moved together, as the dream said, like a single wave through water.

I don't know where my resistance began. It was evident at adolescence, when I rebelled openly, but in some ways it must have been there from the beginning. The creation resists its creator. Otherwise it cannot separate.

Certainly, each time one of her children married, there was a crisis of separation. It was as though she were getting married herself. Because her own family life had been so destructive, she had directed her energy towards one goal, keeping her family together. Even if that meant driving us all away from her.

8

weddings

Her back was a beautiful screen, pink and flushed, a screen that printed emotions. I was reading dread. The white buttons of her department store wedding gown loosened, the dress fell away, peeled back in white wings. My mother on one side, her mother on the other, she knelt in the middle. Not praying, but vomiting. Her back heaved up and down and both mothers in unison cried, "here here," "there there," "calm down." I was speechless. Here was Moira, my wife of a few minutes, in a strange hotel room of plaster putti and ornate sashes.

She'd had too much to drink. A glass of wine at the wedding ceremony had been her first meal of the day. A double martini followed, handed to us by the caterer as we walked into the reception. She threw up after the wedding toast. But the martini did not explain the crying that would not stop and in between the sad ejaculation, "I've ruined my wedding." "If only you'd stop crying," I said uselessly because logically, "you wouldn't be ruining your wedding." No need to tell her: my mother had this effect on all Kamenetz spouses.

I first saw this when my older sister Sonna married a man I'll call Alan Jacobs. The marriage coincided with the launching of his career, which until the age of twenty-seven had lain dormant in his grandmother's basement. There, amidst several miniature railroad systems, he had invented a computer device, DIGIT, Daily Instant Garment Inventory Tally unit. Rigged to a system of sensitized hangers, it was supposed to inventory clothes on the rack. It seemed to me to generate an excitement out of proportion to its mundane capabilities.

Marriage and DIGIT moved on parallel tracks. My father, with the painful vacillations for which he was famous, debated the wisdom of investing in Alan Jacobs' company, while my mother turned the wedding deluxe into a battle royale.

She had decided that the Jacobs considered themselves a cut above the Kamenetzes. That this was true no doubt added to her pique. Their money was older, their neighborhood more exclusive, and they belonged to a country club. Although from any distance at all, one would need a social micrometer to distinguish the two families' status, such differences made all the difference in the world to my mother whose background made her pervious to the least slight.

When we walk through a house, we don't know the hidden meaning of its objects. We are unaware of the invisible radiations emanating from a lamp, a chair, a portrait, or how a casual remark, a tilt of the head, might break those beams, causing doors of hatred and frenzy to fly open. As soon as Elaine Jacobs crossed the threshold of my mother's living room, I heard eggshells cracking. The pine floor, stained dark mahogany and polished to a manic gleam, invited violation, and the large orange rug might have struck Mrs. Jacobs as more than a little overstated. Mr. Jacobs took the direct approach. Puffing rapidly on a cigar thick as a man's forearm, he deposited a sumptuous ash in the center of the rug. The gauntlet thrown down, my mother declared social war.

61

My mother offered "a tour of the house." Alan Jacobs, with long Groucho Marx strides, poked his head into my room. She had made my bed as smooth as icing, straightened my desk beyond recognition, and generally had obliterated all signs of use. On the walls she had framed little certificates I had won in high school. Alan said, "So, this is the room of my dead son."

My parents' desires in the line of marriage had been quite exact. Their daughters were to marry doctors or lawyers, preferably doctors. Alan was neither. He was gawky, with long wrists, shins and neck, an effect which he only emphasized by having his shirts custom-made. He favored high stiff collars with matching large cuffs, both in striped patterns of orange and brown, and asserted with shiny brass collar pins and square silver cufflinks. One saw a huge head poking out of a sharp pointed collar, and long bony veined hands launched into space by exaggerated cuffs.

My father's chief complaint was that Alan had been offered $10,000 and a job at a major electronics firm in exchange for the rights to his invention, but that Alan had turned them down. He wanted to start his own corporation. My father thought this showed a lack of common sense. His doubts found a concrete arena. He was considering investing in the new venture. Alan's stock went up and down the whole time the wedding was being planned. The purchase of a $3000 bond would entitle an investor to 300 shares of stock at a penny a share.

My father eventually took the plunge, deciding to put his money where his daughter was. Having made the decision, he worried more elaborately than before. "Why," he would ask night after night, "haven't the Birnbaums invested?" The Birnbaums were anesthesiologists, and as my father emphasized, "Alan's *own* uncles." Each time Alan crossed our threshold, the same question crossed my father's lips.

My mother looked as though her head had been boiled. Her face seemed to shine crab red and hard-boiled thoughts dominated. At fourteen, I could not follow the intricate details, but the overall atmosphere of tension must have registered on my body: I locked my knees so straight during the wedding ceremony, I keeled over in a faint.

Every day brought a new controversy. There were quarrels over extra invitations, over the engagement party, over snubs and counter-snubs. Who was going to pay? For a year after the happy event, Sonna and my mother did not speak. As younger brother, I became an intermediary, a little white flag sent behind enemy lines. The newlyweds would invite me to dinner, get me drunk, and send the message back to mother: we're doing fine.

My father was in agony. Not only had he invested, but he had persuaded a group of his friends to invest as well. The SEC had recognized the fledgling corporation and given permission for DIGIT to be traded on the open market. The stock went from a penny to nine dollars. My father's friends were pressing for "inside" information. Should they sell? Should they buy more? They hardly believed him when he said he knew nothing.

My father made his living running a drugstore. He concerned himself daily with the price of a box of band-aids, how 2 for 49¢ would stack up against 3 for 67¢. So he was shocked by Alan's success. Here was a company that never, in its brief existence, succeeded in selling a single product. Yet for three years the stock bidding flourished. Greed, and no doubt the wonder of it all, made my father anxious for the inside information his friends were pressing him for, but my mother had cut off the source. Each time I visited the newlyweds, my father would urge me to "pump" Alan, but Alan would only give me a sly smile.

My mother was hurt and bewildered. Since she believed she had acted superbly and that all the wrong was on the Jacobs side, she was willing to be forgiving, but not forgiven. What had driven the newlyweds away, she finally concluded, was my father and his doubts, a theory which while entirely untrue, appeared plausible and shifted blame. Unaware of her own behavior, she was certainly unaware of its causes. She was suffering the pangs of jealousy, for what else would explain a mother's determination to wreck a daughter's wedding?

My mother had always had an intense relation to my twin sisters' dates. She would greet them at the door, she would wait up for them late at night. She'd converse intimately after one of my sisters, yawning, had gone to bed. They were her dates too. They made her ebullient.

My mother liked Alan Jacobs. He was older than most of the twins' dates and had culture, or at least we all thought so since he once presented Sylvia with a complete set of Beethoven Symphonies. But when Alan began dating Sonna, my mother's attitude changed. Her jealousy, and not Leonard Jacobs' cigar ash dropped on the orange rug, prompted her enmity.

I enjoyed my sisters' dates as much as my mother did. If she was searching for a boyfriend, I was in search of a father. Someone had to teach me to play catch. I also served as spy and duenna. While Merrell and Sylvia longed to make out in the living room, I would hang around in my underwear, age ten. If they were going to the library, my mother sent me along in search of books.

My mother would wait each date night for her daughters' return. One night, Sylvia and her date came back in the early hours of the morning. The house was dark and they decided my mother had gone to sleep. As they tiptoed up the porch steps, my mother leapt out of the lawn chair and chased the young man back to his car, swatting him with a broom, and shouting, "Where have you been? It's four in the morning."

Strangely, all of this turmoil made marriage interesting. A little stick of boron, slowing down the radioactive sexuality of my sisters, I had absorbed a tingle of my own. At fifteen I was serious and undyingly devoted in love. The worse I was treated, the better I liked it.

I did not want a woman as a confection, all swirling in crinoline, head floating in a bouffant space capsule. I wanted a pal, an equal. I wanted someone who could tell me who I ought to be and at the same time accept me as I was. In other words, a living contradiction.

I found her in Jane. She was my female equivalent, psychologically. We were like two fragile bits of stemware that vibrated to the same frequency: the music of our affair was high-pitched and resonant. If it wasn't love, it was at least overwhelming.

Well, it wasn't love, or so we decided too late, after we married. I could look into her with complete penetration, and she into me, or so we thought. Of course we saw nothing but ourselves reflected, a narcissism à *deux*. And the disintegration of that harmony made for great dialogues, and produced lots and lots of words, ideal for two poets.

Imagine carrying such fragile glassware into the firestorm of a Kamenetz wedding. If the Jacobs, middle class, Jewish and wealthy, were found unacceptable, what would my mother make of the Carters, Baptists from North Carolina?

She would not let Jane pass without the customary Kamenetz thunder and lightning, even if we planned the ceremony ourselves.

I had brought a new element into the equation. I was marrying a shiksa. I had been dating Gentiles since college. Being younger than most of my class at Yale, desperately horny, pimpled and otherwise undesirable, I took up with the crippled and rejected: women with plastic legs, dwarves, women with six fingers. I tendered them my mutilated passion. What did I care about ancient enmities between Jew and Gentile, about preserving the purity of my cursed blood? During my first three years, Yale was a miserable preserve, an all male college. A monastery punctured by mixers. What could I do at a mixer? The only thing I was good at was talking, which you couldn't do above the music. I danced like a tormented thoroughbred, heaving and snorting, flipping my legs and arms in painful contortions.

I learned the mixer ritual like the stations of the cross: the invitation to dance, the dance, the drink, the second dance, the invitation to the room, the room—and then? I never got that far. I rarely got to the second dance. Even in the dining hall's grimly festive light, a second glance showed most women I was hardly feasible.

Finally Yale went coeducational. At last I had a chance to meet women in classes, in dining halls, on the lawns, to meet them in situations where I could use my mouth, my only attractive feature. But the proverbial nice Jewish girl never seemed to cross my path.

When I married Jane, uppermost in my mind was, what would my grandfather think? I was bringing a shiksa into the family. That was, no doubt, his unspoken thought. I was grateful it remained unspoken.

I had tried to get a rabbi to marry us. But Jane was a feminist, suspicious of the patriarchal nature of Judaism. We decided on religiously neutral ground—the library of Johns Hopkins University. We found a Quaker minister who agreed at my mother's urgent requests never to let the name of Jesus cross his lips. She demanded a copy of the wedding ceremony. She was certain the reverend would try to slip in a JC at the last minute.

We were married beneath a portrait of Milton Eisenhower in his academic regalia. Subtracting Jesus from Christianity did not make the ceremony Jewish. My grandfather saw through the whole charade: that portrait above us, he insisted, was the Pope.

When I escorted my mother down the aisle, she gripped my arm until her knuckles turned white. There were gasps as we entered. She was wearing a white gown.

"It's not really white," she had argued that week to my sisters, to me, to Jane. "It's beige." Perhaps there was a slight hint of yellow in the material. But it was white all right. It was a whammy, a blow from behind; it showed once and for all who was boss. Jane's tears could not change my mother's mind. In the elaborate ceremony, I was called on to serve as my mother's usher. Walking beside her down the aisle, I had the feeling of publicly enacting a dark taboo. I was marrying my mother. What was left? Even Oedipus could plead ignorance.

It is amazing to me that Marx could call for "the abolition of the family" in the Communist Manifesto. For who stands outside a family to abolish it? In our time, the deterioration is inner. Marx thought the family was an economic expression. The only definition of family I can offer is circular. The main idea of the family is, above all, to keep the family together.

Keeping the family together was, in our case, a nearly mystical impulse. Physical proximity mattered. It was betrayal to move from Baltimore. Uncle Louis, my father's older brother, was a near pariah for living in New Jersey. Every holiday he returned, sheepishly. There we were in my grandfather's basement: his four children and their spouses and fourteen grandchildren.

The phrase "nuclear family" has always interested me. The physicists have tried to understand what keeps the various atomic particles from flying apart, and they have come up with "gluons." Whatever gluons are, my grandparents had them. Anyone who came in direct contact with the mystical radiation would stick to the family. I knew intimately all my second and third cousins. I called a pair of boarders my grandparents had in the thirties uncle and aunt. I attended scores of bar mitzvahs, weddings and funerals, brises: my social calendar was so hacked by rites of passage, it bled Manischewitz.

It was love, of course. But not what the troubadours had in mind. Family was a fanning out of a single self into multiple expressions. The family as organism transcended the individual. Grandmother Kamenetz had Napoleonic ambitions. To her, "family" meant an entire "family circle." This was the name of an organization she invented. This family of families met once a month in various locations in Maryland and Pennsylvania, and included all the descendants of Morris and Leah Singer, a nearly mythical patriarchal couple who were my grandmother's grandparents. My grandmother's father, Henry Singer, had brought them from the old country for their golden wedding anniversary. They lived to celebrate their diamond. Longevity is a great aid to family cohesion.

The extended family made immigration possible. The family was health, welfare and aid society. It was bank and Jewish community center. So intense was the knotting, with cousins marrying cousins, that people ended up related to each other in complex ways.

The marriage of first cousins was quite common in my grandparents' generation, and there were the predictable genetic results. But it merely illustrates the exclusivity of the family unit, the intensity with which family connections were sought. And the isolation of the immigrant generation. Who else was there, outside of family?

In Baltimore, the circumscription was reinforced by geography. The "neighborhood" was a world apart. My father still speaks proudly of the old Druid Park, the brick rowhouses with rounded towers and turrets, the lake, the zoo, the corner drugstore, the shul. The ghetto was a ghetto by choice. For him, there was no yearning for the outside world, no sense of isolation. After World War II, my father's generation, scattered all over the globe, came back and carried the ghetto into the raw suburbs.

Forest Hill Road, where I grew up, was a ghetto, at least the new parts of the block were where the developer had bulldozed a "forest hill" and built brick tract homes. Up the street, close to Liberty Road, the Gentiles lived in white frame houses. But we never had much to do with them, nor they with us.

I never grew up with a sense of inferiority. To be a Jew seemed natural. I can remember only one anti-Semitic incident in my childhood, and a mild one at that. I was walking in the Gentile part of the block (in my childish geography), and a boy blocked my path and said, "You Jew." I was twelve. I remember a long pause. I had time to wonder, "Should I consider this an insult?" After all, I *was* a Jew. However, the tone was quite clear, so, on reflection, I punched him in the nose.

Up the street were the Levis, Czech Jews who had both survived the concentration camps. I'd seen the tattoos on their arms, but what impressed me most was the red Corvette parked in their driveway.

We lived outside the tragic history of the Jewish people. I never experienced being Jewish as abject, never experienced the self-loathing common among victims of prejudice. I was simply puzzled by Jews who changed their names. Why would anyone persecute people as intelligent, lively and friendly as we? I lived an idyll.

Weddings make entire families nervous. A marriage always holds the potential of breaking a family apart. In the earlier years, my older sisters and cousins were obliged to bring their new mates to "meet the family." At Passover or Chanukah, the newcomer would be carefully inspected and commented on. It was important that the family liked him. It was equally important that he like the family. His qualifications were openly discussed: "a Harvard man," "a lawyer," "his father is rich." It was a shock many potential suitors did not survive.

My mother, as guardian of our nuclear family and chief center around which the Kamenetzes orbited, was particularly sensitive to any new additions. This accounted for the scathing rites of passage she inflicted on each new mate. To enter her domain one had to be humbled. Was it worth it?

I thought I could avoid the whole issue by marrying outside the faith. A Gentile was unacceptable by definition, therefore would not be attacked personally. Perhaps that was my logic. What I wanted, above all, was to marry someone who was not my mother. To marry a Jewish woman would have been too much like incest.

Jane and I had a restless marriage. During its three years we moved around—California, North Carolina, back to Baltimore. We separated in the summer of 1976, and I met Moira soon after.

By the time I married Moira, my mother was quite ill. My engagement, marriage, the birth of my first child, ran parallel to her secondary tumors, her final operations, her dying. Still, with perverse will power, she managed to inject plenty of tension into the proceedings. It almost made me sad to see how mild her efforts were, compared to previous campaigns. Just a few squabbles over guest lists and flowers. But perhaps great troublemakers, like great artists, learn an economy of means.

She insisted at the last minute that we should invite her friends instead of my cousins. She wanted to punish the cousins who had not visited her in the hospital and reward the friends who had.

My mother's machinations were making Moira nervous. She could accept converting to Judaism. She was more nervous about becoming a Kamenetz. I couldn't blame her. I was alive to the possibilities of catastrophe my mother could engender. But I was also afraid she would die. It wouldn't seem like a wedding without her. I was a veteran of insane tension, but it was getting to Moira. For weeks, she couldn't eat or sleep.

The wedding made her sick to her stomach. She missed everything but the final dance. She kept repeating over and over, "I've ruined my wedding, I've ruined everything," and breaking out in deep sobs that shook her body all over. I realized how profound a transformation I had demanded of her. It was tearing her apart. This was not a wedding, but a birth. When she had swallowed the ceremonial wine, she had imbibed a magic potion of ambivalence and foreign tragedy.

And so, staring at her heaving back, I was moved. I tried to calm her, but my words were flying far overhead. Only hours later, when the band had played the Hava Nagila, when everyone else, oblivious to our absence, had eaten and drunken their fill, danced themselves silly, when my father-in-law found himself lifted on a chair and carried around in Hasidic fashion, did we emerge. Pale, drained, nervous, drab smiles plastered on our faces, or so the photographs show, we danced a little dance and slipped away. We were married.

If my mother, sick and dying, could have such effects on us as adults, think what she could do to us as children. My mother's will had a ruinous intensity. Its strength made me weak.

9

the will

"You can do anything," my mother had always told me. Anything was in many ways such a large and glorious prospect, it seemed specificity could only diminish it. I felt like a large block of marble waiting for the master's chisel. For years I was dazzled by my own potential. Anything! Who'd dare knock off a chip?

I lived anything, knew anything, and above all believed anything.

Until I graduated from Yale, I was my mother's main chance. She believed in me because she never imagined believing in herself. I tried every strategy to elude her good opinion.

She had made a career of being a mother. She had given it inordinate energy. I was dazed by the extra attention like a body burnt by too much sun. I was embarrassed by her love, that deep embarrassment a child has when he feels himself turning into an object. Yet I was in a double bind. It would be churlish to refuse her praise. It was going the only place it could go, to my head.

"Come on, can't you pitch in?" she would sometimes ask, picking up the socks and shoes from under my feet.

"Full of potential," I was too heavy to move. The idea of cooperating with anyone seemed especially dreadful; it would bruise my possibilities. I might lose that special aura that set me apart. All of this would have made much more sense if I weighed three hundred pounds. I was skinny. Most of my energy went into scheming ways to avoid moving.

I became a poet at age fifteen. I decided after reading Rimbaud's *Illuminations*. At last there was something that could *not* be understood. I pledged myself to the glamour of this magic language that negated the boredom of middle class certainties. Charleville was the ultimate suburb, but Rimbaud had found the formula for "eluding happiness, which no one can escape."

By sixteen set loose in college, I had discovered the "*dérèglement de tous les sens*" with a vengeance. Rimbaud and William Blake were my mentors; "The Proverbs of Hell" was my syllabus. "The road of excess leads to the palace of wisdom," I told anyone who would listen. In May of 1968, I earned a few hundred dollars working as a janitor; in June I hitchhiked across the Mojave Desert. I returned to Baltimore broke with nothing to do but sit on my bed.

Waves were coming out of the wall, waves of fear that struck me in the stomach and nauseated me. No use discussing that with Mom and Dad. How to explain the time that spring I inhaled LSD up my nose? The local irritation merged into the insane idea that I was going to drown in my own mucus. That night, climbing West Rock, I had seen a burst of lightning slowly squeeze out of a cloud for what seemed an hour. By early morning, an agony of waiting for the drug to wear off. Instead of tick-tock-tick-tock, the world's clock had melted: tick, glob, slush . . .

My mother was most upset that her genius, her sunshine boy, had found his life's work as a janitor. I did not mind the lack of status. In fact, to be a janitor exactly expressed my antinomian politics. I learned from Bobby and Mack, the two regular janitors, blacks who thought I was crazy, how to clean a window properly. I inhaled the faint blue soapy aroma of Windex. I learned the secret lore of sweeping, using the edge of the broom sidewise to catch the finer particles.

I didn't know I was repeating the life of Benjamin, her father. The man of Talmud had become a barber. With the kabala of Rimbaud, I was janitor, dishwasher.

None of my professors at Yale could tell me what it meant to be a poet. They looked at me as an oddity. My poet friends simply shrugged off my questions about money. "Come to New York," they told me. "Go on your nerve." But I just got nervous.

They were quoting their idol, and mine, Frank O'Hara. Deliberately trivial, witty, light-hearted, urban and urbane, above all roughened by the hard edges of city life, O'Hara's bright poems were instructions on how to live as well as how to write: in many ways they were the same. I memorized phrases from his manifesto on Personism: "You just go on your nerve. If someone's chasing you down the street with a knife you just run, you don't turn around and shout, 'Give it up! I was a track star for Mineola Prep.'"

But Yale had swollen my ego, made it bulky and unmaneuverable. As I walked the streets of New York in search of a typing job, I tried to keep the cheerful spirit of Frank O'Hara beside me: *Pain produces logic which is very bad for you. It is only when you stop thinking that the refreshment arrives.* But I couldn't stop thinking about myself. The streets of New York looked dirty, bleak and expensive; there was no money for lunch with Leroi or to shop "for bargains in wristwatches" and anyway, Leroi had changed his name to Amiri Baraka and was somewhere in Newark. 515 Madison

Avenue, "the heaven on earth building," had been torn down. I was spoiled and impatient. I wanted New York to send me an admissions letter, like the one I'd gotten from Yale.

1970. Six months earlier at the height of the May Day demonstrations at Yale, I had been convinced I was at the center of history. I felt I was going to graduate into the apocalypse. After Nixon and Kissinger invaded Cambodia, millenarianism abounded. Somehow, though, the end of the world failed to arrive in time to save me from myself. The demonstrators left the campus, the class of '70 graduated as classes had graduated before, and New Haven's brief moment in "the revolution" passed as well. I joined a group of holdouts in a "Black Panther Revolutionary Poetry Commune," a rather baroque title for a summer sublet. We were glum. A calm descended on the Yale campus. June frisbees sailed over manicured lawns where, a month before, I had watched Allen Ginsberg chanting OM through clouds of tear gas.

I had no idea how to look for a job. Instead of job descriptions, I had job proscriptions. I would not work for the government that perpetrated the war in Vietnam. I would not work for any major American corporation, all complicit with racism. And thanks to Richard Nixon's recession, I would not work at all.

That fall, a friend lent me his floor to sleep on in the Upper West Side. I had five dollars to my name. Every morning I would go to the New York public library to look at the want ads since I couldn't afford a newspaper. Across Fifth Avenue were several job agencies where I submitted to a few interviews—there was nothing.

One night I found myself on the Staten Island ferry, crossing dark water. I walked to the edge of the boat with thoughts of Hart Crane. But basically I was a coward; I suffered from a certain literalness of imagination. I hated the thought of the garbage flocked East River, the filth and oil scum floating in my nostrils.

Soon I was living with my parents. I was twenty years old, and the sixties had collapsed. My parents soon grew tired of watching their expensively educated son lying on his back watching "I Love Lucy," so I hastily picked a new career—publishing. I wrote two dozen letters, introducing myself to the New York literary world as a promising young man. I was beginning to promise everything.

My mother made one last attempt to save me. She brought out her ace in the hole, Cousin Reg. An urbane and sophisticated Englishman, he had come to America and made his way in the advertising world. He knew influential people, including Norman Cousins, the editor of the *Saturday Review*.

Reg wrote and advised me to familiarize myself with Cousins and his magazine. I was going to have a personal job interview. Cousins, I gathered, had three main hobbyhorses. First, he was a one-worlder. He believed in "the Jeffersonian democracy of nations," a rather hopeful, though ethnocentric notion. He had two other obsessions. Fighting yawns, I read his hosannas for Albert Schweitzer, and his jeremiads against air pollution. Norman Cousins was sincere. Sincerity is often dull. The more I read, the more I disliked his safe, reasonable views, and the safe reasonable art his magazine championed.

Still, I was impressed when I found myself in a fancy office building in Manhattan. I had a haircut for the occasion and a suit and tie. I felt twitchy, *"mal dans le peau,"* uncomfortable in my skin. When I got off the elevator, my mouth was dry and sweat was pooling under my arms. This was it: the big interview, the big connection—my certain entrée into the publishing world.

"Rodger Kamenetz—I'd like to see Mr. Cousins?" I squeaked uncertainly to the formidable secretary.

"What did you say?" she demanded in a loud voice, standing up. She was approximately eight feet tall. I thought she was going to pick me up by my hairy neck and toss me out of the office.

"I have an appointment," I added weakly. "Kamenetz?" All my statements trailed off into questions.

"Oh yes, Mr. Kamenetz, take a seat."

Doors opened and closed and beautiful young women in plaid skirts and silk blouses rustled past me. It would be great to work here, I decided. I could overcome my distaste for the review; I could change the magazine for the better.

I rehearsed: "Love your magazine." "Schweitzer." "The Jeffersonian democracy of nations!"

Norman Cousins was bald and wore a bow tie. He had a wrinkled brow and the air of a librarian.

"What can I do for you?" he asked.

"Give me a job immediately," I felt like saying. Instead I stuttered a confused and idiotic sentence to the effect that I had always admired the *Saturday Review*, a sad lie that shamed my soul. I noticed his windows were smudged. That reminded me of air pollution. How terrible it was. How it was ruining our cities. He stared grimly. I was blowing the interview. It seemed slaver was running from the corners of my mouth and puddling in the heels of my shoes. My eyes fell on a bust of Albert Schweitzer. I started gibbering about the Saint of Lambarané.

"Yes," Cousins said. What else could he say?

"And the Jeffersonian democracy of nations!" I began. He nodded his head. Finally, I stopped. Maybe I'd been a little nervous at first, but I felt I'd recovered brilliantly.

"The *Saturday Review*," Cousins began, "has a very wide and sophisticated readership."

77

Great, I thought, he's telling me about the job.

"Our advertising section gets an enormous response."

I nodded. He was going to give me a start in the advertising section.

"So if you'd like, perhaps you could run an ad in the next issue, with my compliments."

My mother never understood my failures. She was disappointed I hadn't become somebody "great, like Henry Kissinger." After all, I'd gone to Yale. All doors were open for me. She didn't realize that all I'd opened in New Haven were the doors of perception.

I bounced around for a couple of years, holding odd jobs in odd cities: Syracuse, New Haven, Pittsburgh. I ended up in Baltimore but began to sense a coolness from my mother. One day my brother told me, "She's given up on you." At last I had succeeded in failing.

Once I saw that, I was free. All the painful turning and twisting had been an elaborate birth ritual. I had painfully separated myself from my parents. I was trying to become something they had no adequate idea of, a poet. I decided to make my escape, to leave for Mexico. The night I left, my mother said, "Okay, you want to be a poet. Why don't you do something practical with your writing?" "What?" I said. "Why not write pornography?"

So I was off to Mexico. I thought to break free at last. I flew to New Orleans in February. Jane saw me off. She promised to meet me in the Yucatán in May. Meanwhile, I made my way by bus to Mexico City.

A few weeks later, my mother's doctor discovered bleeding in her bowels. The doctors came to her and said this: We would like to operate on you. We would like to remove several feet of your colon, on either side of the tumor that you have. We would like to make a hole in your abdomen and attach a plastic bag there, out of which you will shit for the rest of your life. If you let us do this, we can promise you a 60 per cent chance of surviving. If you don't, your odds are less than one out of three.

This was the decision she met alone. She was too proud to listen to anyone around her.

If my mother could have read the book of her own life to the end, I know she would have chosen differently.

But she never saw her prospects. She would be the one to outwit the odds.

My mother saw herself living every day in the stink of her own shit, as though fate had contrived an adequate symbol for her past. She had spent her whole life separating herself from this shit. And now they were going to tie it back around her.

Given her character, what could she do? What she'd instilled in me, she believed herself. "You can do anything." She had to defy the doctors, defy her fate.

Given her character . . . At the same time I was in Mexico. I had established myself in a rooftop apartment in the Zona Rosa, the pink zone, of Mexico City. I was learning Spanish, writing poems. I loved my life. I was on my own. I didn't want to think any more about my mother and her sad ambitions for me.

After a month, I was ready to leave the capitol, to explore the ruins. I had been studying every day in the library of the Museo Antropológico, and I was ready to go. I decided to call my parents before I left. I went to Sanborn's, the drugstore hangout for Americans in Mexico City. It took hours to get to the phone. There were only a few long distance lines and all the Americans were waiting their turn. At last when I got through, my parents sounded distant. My father said something about doctors' checkups and my mother said there was nothing wrong—sure sign that something was.

I heard a lie, then, over the telephone lines. But I turned my back on it. I didn't want to be pulled back to her. I didn't want them to ruin my new sense of myself as a poet. My mother didn't want to force me to abandon my trip, yet she must have hoped that even the faint hint, which I did receive in the way her voice seemed to quaver, would pique my curiosity enough to question her more closely.

I have no excuse for what I did. What I knew, I repressed immediately. I was thinking of her and not thinking of her, in that strange way we deny. How had I become so cold towards my mother? I was more her creature than was comfortable for me to imagine and fled the power she had over me.

I left Mexico City for the ruins, traveling for weeks along the Pacific coast, then up from Puerto Escondido north. One day I arrived in Oaxaca. There was a postcard waiting for me from my sister. The postcard said that my mother was having an operation for a tumor. She didn't want me to know, but my sister thought I should.

I felt angry at my sister for telling me. I felt angry at my mother for not. I acted with a cold heart. I folded the postcard in my pocket and went on.

My girlfriend was coming to Mexico. Jane was going to meet me on May 5 at five P.M. in the main square of Merida. Surely I could not change those plans. Besides, by the time I'd received the card, the operation was done, for better or worse.

So I went on. But I kept the postcard and one day, a few years later, my mother found it among my papers. Weeping, she brought it to me and said, "So you knew."

It was like my Aunt Rachel saying, "You were never there when I needed you."

I might have saved her. Not a strong chance, given my own confusion, but I might have been the one to see clearly, might have been the one whose bond was strong enough to make her see what she had to do. I don't know, I can't know.

What could I have done had I been there? When my mother learned of her tumor, and of her choice, the doctors told her that there was only one conservative course. A tumor in the bowel had to be removed with as much surrounding tissue as possible.

In this sense, a colon cancer was one of the luckier ones because there were so many feet of intestine that could be safely cut away. But it meant cutting through the rectum. It meant wearing a colostomy bag.

My mother would not accept the "conservative" opinion. She found out about a doctor in Cleveland who'd had success with partial surgery. She screamed, she argued; basically, she refused to cooperate. In the end, very reluctantly, her surgeon was persuaded to take a chance.

The danger of the procedure my mother wanted was this: a single cell would be enough to start the tumor in the colon again. Worse, the primary tumors could metastasize, spreading to other parts of the body. Colon cancers often travel to the liver or the brain.

Up until the day of the operation, my mother's doctor tried to persuade her to the conservative course. So did my father and sisters. She defied them. In the glory of her defiance, she became convinced she could beat the odds. She could do anything! Besides, she said, she'd rather die than wear a colostomy bag.

That's what it all came down to.

My father says that even as they were wheeling her into the O.R., the surgeons were giving her a permission form to sign. She refused.

Could I have persuaded her differently? Could I have shown her that it was better to live with an inconvenience than to die of a shame? Did she think enough of herself to make such a decision?

Her defiance was not pride, but its lack. She felt herself too small to bear such a stain. She could not accept the possibility of imperfection in her life. She separated herself from it fastidiously.

As she went into surgery, they told her, "You're tying our hands." When she came out, they said, "We got all of it." Yet every three months she was "put on the table." The physician probed inside her for any sign of tumor. She lived her life in short reprieves.

For a few years after that first operation the gamble seemed to have paid off. No sign was found of any new growth. If she passed her physical for three years, she would be pronounced cured.

In the meantime, she changed. She seemed to be flowering in her life. The willfulness that she had used to defy the doctors, and to control her family, she was now using on the world.

She became ambitious. She went after the education she'd been deprived of. She wanted to recuperate in every sense.

She was not an easygoing student. She sat in the front of the class, took voluminous notes and demanded conferences. I don't believe any instructor at the college was capable of resisting her. She may not have been the most brilliant student, unless determination is itself a form of brilliance, but she moved through her classes with matchless force. The energy she had used to push five children through school was now pushing her. She wanted the world to stamp her as A-material. The day she got her degree was a triumph.

She looked for work. Her illness propelled her. She claimed she was attracted to medical work though she had no talent for science. Her choice of jobs was symbolic. If she worked for a doctor, by primitive reasoning she could not be sick.

As a secretary for a group of radiologists, she soon re-

82

organized the whole office. The doctors liked her, she said. They took her out to lunch. After a few months, my mother told us how she "ran the office." She was more than just a secretary. She was practically an associate. In a few more days, she was fired.

How could they fire Miriam, the indispensable? She had meddled too much in the doctors' business. They didn't want an equal, they wanted a secretary.

She cried for two days and found another job. There was always "room at the top" as she had told me so many times.

She lost her second job simply because she wanted her title changed to Executive Secretary. She liked the sound of "executive." Her boss was all too aware of what such a concession might mean.

But her disease pulled her up short. At one of her check-ups, the doctor discovered a new growth of tumor. Her gamble had not paid off. This time she was more scared. She was willing, after all, to put up with a colostomy.

As it turned out, the colostomy wasn't needed. The tumor was alarming though, the size of a lime. She recovered remarkably. Her body was working against her now, but her will was very muscular. She had prodded and pushed my father and me and my brothers and sisters through life. Now she was going to push herself.

Meanwhile, I was struggling. My trip to Mexico had given me a vision, but I didn't know what to do with it. I lived in San Francisco on thirty-five dollars a week and went to graduate school at Stanford. I managed a seedy apartment building in Palo Alto, then dropped out after reading *Walden*. Married to Jane, we lived on a thousand-acre soybean farm in North Carolina. I was in agony, a nobody, a half-born poet. "Je" might be "un autre." But all I was was what I was not.

My grandfather died, and Jane and I came back to Baltimore. Our marriage collapsed. Alone, I began to think about my grandfather, my father's father. I discovered I could write poems in his voice, poems that first came to me in dictation in a dream. I went back through the voice of my grandfather, to the voices of all the grandfathers, those dead Hebrew spirits who were constant immigrants and wanderers. I wrote a book, *The Missing Jew*.

I was a poet in the city where I had been born, where my parents had named me a failure. There was an odd irony in it—I was celebrating them. That's not what I'd expected when I started with Rimbaud, at fifteen. I had been looking for a way out, a way to escape the dullness around me. I had learned in Mexico that I had to start from death before I could get any further. I had established myself by taking a step backward, generationally, positioning myself in the time before my parents. Their parents were the strong ones. My father's father had arrived with nothing, and he had made his own way.

My voice was on the radio, my poems were in the air, *The Missing Jew* was published. I was commissioned by a synagogue to write a series of poems to be set to music. I had doubts about the project. *The Missing Jew* had been a pure gesture of self-definition. The cantata seemed a compromise. Yet I knew it would please my parents. At the same time it would force them to acknowledge I was a poet, in the sight of their friends and neighbors.

All that time my mother was dying. Two weeks after the doctors pronounced her "cured," her headaches began. The doctor attributed them to tension, blood pressure. Could it be an abscess? Then we knew the truth. The cancer had metastasized, traveling through her bloodstream to her cerebellum.

In her hospital room, reviews of my first book were tacked on her wall. An article appeared about the cantata I had written. A thousand people were expected for the performance. She wanted to hear it. By now her body had completely betrayed her. Tumors in her brain, her spine, her liver—she could not eat without vomiting, or move without great pain. She had tried every cure, radiation that blasted her hair, chemotherapy that ruined her memory, and now all the doctors could give her were larger and larger doses of painkiller that disoriented her, made her feel she was floating on the ceiling. No matter. She was going to attend the performance.

There was no way to get her there. Her spine, eaten by tumor, could shatter at the slightest blow. No medical van would take the risk.

She asked who was going to take her. She announced to me that she was going.

A few hours before the performance, I went to see her. I told her I would make a tape. She told me if I wouldn't help her, she'd find a way on her own.

A newspaper article in the Baltimore *Sun* had packed the synagogue. I was nervous. As the choir sang the first notes, heads turned to the back. My mother was riding down the center aisle in a gurney chair. Her face was broken with tears. My brother and sister were pushing her. Why people were staring was obvious. My mother had left her deathbed. No makeup could camouflage her condition.

I was stunned. She had done it for me. The next morning at the hospital, she lay motionless. When I thanked her, she would not, or could not, answer.

When I say my mother's life flowered after her first operation, I think also of those flowers in the hospice garden, those strange white tulips of her death. They were also flowers of her will. Though I will always cherish the great strength that brought her literally off her deathbed, for my sake—I also know that same will power caused her to die sooner than she needed to.

In her pride, she'd risked her life foolishly, made the wrong decision, taken the wrong operation. In that sense, her extraordinary will was a tragic flaw. And she suffered, in her body, all its painful consequences.

10

terra infirma

Her face was swollen and on one side flushed with in-
jected dye. Stubble surrounded a plastic bubble on the top
of her head. Her hair had grown back curly after the radiation treatments, a mild gray like ash. She held her back
stiffly and when she stood, she felt pain in the back of her
neck that seemed to emanate from the purple surgical scar.

She stood with great difficulty. She liked to sit in stiff
wooden chairs with pillows cushioning her back. When she
wished to stand, she held out her arms, somnambulist-
style and I would help lift her, for her legs were weak.
Sometimes she would get stuck halfway. There would be a
panic in her eyes then and I would pull hard to get her up.
"Oooh-oooh," she would cry, almost comically, but it was
pain. When she had straightened all the way, she would
rest in my arms from the effort. Then, steadied, she'd
shuffle off by herself, leaving her walker. She'd hold the
walls for support.

Her feet were quite swollen. You could no longer make
out her ankle bones, the skin ballooned over them. My father had split a pair of black lace-ups and fit them around
her feet, taping up the sides with bandages.

The Decadron kept her alive by squeezing fluid from her

tumors. But the fluid settled in her feet and legs. It was like walking with your shoes full of water. Her body was so swollen her cheeks cracked and bled. Beneath her skin, in neat scripture, her veins wrote red and thin.

She fell twice. First in the kitchen. My brother heard her head hit the counter edge with a smack. He came running over to where she lay on the floor. She was bleeding heavily above the right eye.

I saw her the next day. She had done what she could to repair herself. She had the old rituals to protect her. She peered into a magnifying mirror, combing patches of hair, then tied a kerchief to cover her skull. Her face was perfectly round now from the swelling of her cheeks. Both eyes were black from the fall; she covered them over with flesh-tint makeup. She wrapped a bandage over the cut, a little thickly, and asked me to trim it with manicure scissors, as a flap was troubling her vision.

"I'm going out tonight to a surprise party."

Two days later I saw her again. The "surprise party" had gone badly for her.

"They stared at me," she said. Her voice had gotten as small as a child's calling out from a well.

She hated those eyes. Eyes of disapproval, eyes coldly measuring her and registering her appearance. She saw a depth to surfaces, an implied social order. My mother believed in the aristocracy of good looks. She was born to nothing. She owed no allegiance to hidden treasures. She owed all her loyalty to what appeared to the eye. I don't believe she was vain. To my mother, appearances were not deceiving, they were glorifying. What she found in the right dress, the right "outfit," was herself.

My mother never went out without dressing herself completely two times. I remember my childhood as an involuntary spectator at a fashion show. "How do I look?" But no matter how enthusiastic I pretended to be, she would always turn back, with disappointment, turn back to the mirror, the dressing table, the closet, and begin again. My father could tap his foot, point to his watch, stalk back and forth in the living room with his overcoat on, but his time was only by the clock. She was creating a different time, one in which she could emerge, perfumed, furred, marvelous. The delay was part of the presentation, a ripple in time. And so as my father would grab her arm at last, and huff, "We're late," the emphasis was lost in her knowing smile. She was beautiful. How could she be "late"?

This was my mother in full confidence. When depressed, she would lounge for days in a ratty brown bathrobe. Pale her lips without their cheery red and sad her eyes with smeared and faded eye shadow. Like a rag doll on the shelf, she slumped in the corner of the sofa.

Going out was all important. Even at the last stages of her illness, she took it as a challenge. Her hair may have fallen out completely, but that did not prevent her from wearing a jaunty Spanish bolero hat, with a red ribbon for accent. If others stared, she ignored them as much as she could, but if they stared too long or too hard, she would lash out furiously.

There seemed to be a club among the dying. A senile old fossil would toddle up to her at a party and ask her bluntly, "What's wrong with you?" as if happy to see someone going in ahead of her. And my mother would reply, "I'm in excellent condition, but you look terrible. Have you seen your doctor lately?"

No matter how bad such moments, going out was a game worth the candle. It gave her something to look forward to. It was a refuge from staying home where one might get depressed or be lonely or helpless. That's why the surprise party so depressed her. It was really the last party.

A week later she fell again. No one was home. She fell

out of bed in the morning and got her head wedged between the mattress and an old trunk she was using for a night stand. It took her an hour to extricate herself.

I moved the trunk further from the bed. It was no wonder she'd fallen. Because of the pain in her back and spine, she had pillows stacked three deep under the mattress, so that she slept like someone reading in bed. At the same time, to allay the swelling in her ankles, she had another stack of pillows at the foot of the bed.

She said, "That fall was a real setback to me, but I had a good day today."

When I read my own account of what happened to my mother's body, I cannot do so without pain. I had thought these words might have lost their power in time, but they hurt more today than when the notes were first written. Perhaps writing then was a relief from the experience. The very mechanics of writing are soothing when I am lost in the subject; the movement of my fingers at the typewriter or the rote scratching of a pen on paper occupies the most nervous and self-conscious part of my body, my hands, and the concentration required shuts out the world and erases time.

Only when the writing is going badly is it painful. The subject will not stay still and the words do not hold together. Each word is a different cut.

When I have my subject though, it is round and full, a body at my hands. Its contours extend in a familiar shape, I feel its fullness as a certainty and am eager to get the words that will hold it before it gets away. It is as though I am carrying someone in my body, someone precious who will either come out clean or botched.

I think too with my body. And yet I don't firmly believe in its existence. That is, when I am happy I believe in it, and when I am lost I can't find it.

What is hard here is to find my mother's sufferings on

my own body. In thinking about them, in describing them, they are always going abstract, lightening, turning into the words that describe them.

When my father wished so much for me to be a doctor, the only argument I ever found that he respected was my "weak stomach." But that is a distortion. It is not true that I am squeamish. I can stand the sight of blood. What I can't stand is to hear it described.

Once in Palo Alto walking an overpass, I looked down and saw a strange sight. A man was lying on his back in the middle of the road, his head resting neatly on the centerline. There was no sign of traffic, nothing to indicate how he had gotten there. I hurried down to him and saw blood trickling from the back of his head. I felt quite calm.

Only later, when I told the anecdote, when I described the blood puddling in the dust, the pulsing of a vein beneath his eye socket, I began to feel ill.

"Our own death," Freud said in 1915, "is indeed unimaginable." Yet I think the reason I do feel ill is that I imagine myself lying in the road, imagine my blood trickling past my ear.

If a friend describes to me his kidney stones, I immediately locate an intense pain in what I imagine to be my left kidney. I feel the pain in my urethra though I don't know exactly where it is, feel a large rough salty stone passing slowly down a tube below my waist. And on my face I have the most hypocritically good countenance but I wonder that he can't see behind my smile that my lips are pale, my forehead is white and that I am about to faint.

I don't have an extraordinarily accurate idea of anatomy. But I feel another's pain moving through my body. And then my heart pounds, my breath comes short and fast, and it is very important that I sit down.

Language sets it off. After my mother's second operation, my sister and I were waiting for her return from a surgery. They wheeled her through the doors, tubes in her nose, the surgeon following close behind in his green gown, unbuttoned at the shoulder, his cap pushed back on his brow.

"How big was it?" my sister was moved to ask.

"The size of a lime."

That did it for me. I had been handling it well, but the picture of the tumor was now so vivid, I felt I could see blood pooling on the tile. I looked back at my mother. There were black hairs and grey hairs tousled on her forehead and great balls of sweat, her eyelids pale and cold . . . It was no use. I fell to a crouch, leaned against the wall, and lowered my head.

The surgeons always seem to answer with weird incongruity, in terms of fruit or nuts. "The size of an almond," this for a brain tumor that drove a man mad. "The size of a grapefruit" for a horror removed from a woman's belly.

I don't know what interest my mother's suffering could have to a reader. I've imagined sometimes that describing it in great detail might have a socially useful function. Other times I can't imagine what it is. Who wants to feel exactly what it is like to die?

Montaigne writes that the vulgar cannot think about death, that they cannot even say the word without crossing themselves, that the ancient Romans could not bring themselves to say simply, he died, but rather, he has lived. It is impossible to imagine our own deaths, and Freud remarks, when we do try, we always imagine ourselves as spectators. Who has not dreamed of dying? But always it is to attend one's own funeral and see the reactions of others. To imagine oneself as a thing is nearly impossible. It is far easier to imagine that dust can think, than to truly know I will be dust under another's feet.

Yet, Montaigne instructs us, we must think of our death at all times. Think of it, think of it, yet I cannot think of it, or cannot think of it properly. I know I am going to die. But there is knowing and knowing. I do not know I am going to die palpably, the way I know the taste of a lemon before I bite into it.

I don't believe it would do me any good to acquire a skull or lie in a coffin as John Donne was said to have done, swaddled in shrouds. I have great "life expectancy," a phrase I am sure would have amused Montaigne, who knew himself an old man at thirty-nine, and chided himself for waiting so long to think about his death.

When I think of her face, her eyes in panic, her cheek bruised, the cut above her right eye, the sharp smacking sound as her forehead hit the counter . . .

It is the strangest thing that we have bodies, that we are not round and transparent like drops of water. And stranger too that the body has an inside and an outside, an outside that can be seen and an inside that can only be known secondhand.

It is eerie sometimes to be sitting quietly reading, and then to hear a soft gurgling sound and feel a fluid racing through a passageway somewhere just below the belly. The body going on about its business. But my body? And yet one feels so dissociated from the movement of that fluid. I did not command it to move, I did not know it would happen. I have no certain knowledge of why it is moving, what message it might carry, what meaning, if any, it might have.

Blake says, perhaps too easily, the body is the soul. But what of the body in pain, diseased, damaged? Is that my soul? If I were to be operated on and could see the operation in a mirror, I believe I could do so with nearly clinical indifference. That stuffing inside, those organs, would be like any organs. I could not call them mine, they would not be personal. I could not say, this is my heart, this is my bladder, in the same way I say, these are my hands.

I remember standing next to my mother as she sat in her stiff-backed chair, and running my fingers through her hair. So soft and woolly, like Blake's lamb, and I thought also of:

. . . little Tom Dacre who cried when his head
That curl'd like a lamb's back, was shav'd: so I said
"Hush Tom! never mind it, for when your head's bare
You know that the soot cannot spoil your white hair."

The radiation treatments had made it all fall out, but it had grown back in short clumps, stiff and curly. I touched it gingerly as though hair, too, could feel pain.

One makes the same complaints of disease and literature. If only it were easier to read. If only its aesthetics weren't so constantly ironic. If only the experts could clarify the obscurities. Yet the very act of interpreting can alter the message: drugs can mask symptoms, treatments can create side effects more terrible than the disease, or even, in my mother's case, one pain can mask another far worse.

The family also tries its hand at interpretation. They go it alone, without expertise or distance, they read fearfully, tenderly. Every change in the body is a change in their own flesh and blood. What information can be gleaned from the pronouncements of doctors, the chance remarks of nurses and orderlies, or the phrases in a medical textbook—is studied passionately. The body, the family's concern—these are the constants as the illness progresses. Externally, a kaleidoscope of doctors, nurses, settings, treatments: internally, a constant fear, a hollow feeling, and the need to fill that hollow with information, interpretation, speculation. So we read my mother's illness.

The phrase is strange. "My mother's illness"—as though it belonged somehow to her, like her eyes. Yet one cannot help seeing it that way after living with it. The illness becomes a feature of the person, in many ways, the dominant feature. It is the fact that organizes everything. Chiefly it organizes time into a dramatic landscape. Sharply etched cliffs with steep descents provide views of valleys below. And then, caverns, holes slashed in the earth, abysses with underground passages and black cold rivers. It is *terra infirma*, shaky ground.

When the patient is forced to confront her own death, a dizzying perspective opens up: she stands on a cliff, and her loved ones stand beside her, looking down on the panorama of a life. It is breathtaking and produces a philosophical calm, as the Chinese sages knew who came to the mountains to die.

Dostoevsky experienced such a moment: blindfolded, against a wall, believing he was about to be executed by a firing squad. The command was given, the rifles were fired, and then, nothing. The bullets were blanks, there was a reprieve, a terrible joke was played. A joke that changed his life profoundly. So, in his novels, time is compressed; there is a constant frenzy and the sense that at any moment, all of this might end. All the characters talk as though this were the last night on earth, as though tomorrow a page would turn and they would be no more: their elaborate speeches are squeezed out at great pressure; I find the intensity of reading *The Brothers Karamazov*, for instance, nearly unbearable. I shake, I pace the room, my body seems to have become a conductor for the book's electricity, and the foreshortening of time which is the essence of the novel, years condensed into pages read in hours—becomes a physical sensation as well.

When my mother told us the story of her life, she believed she would die the next day in surgery. And when she woke from the operation, it was with astonishment.

She grabbed our hands, she looked from face to face, she could not consider that all this was real, that she had returned to the bright world.

My mother's illness became after a time, that fiction, "the story of her life." It was like a book we all were reading and discussing, a book we treated as a mystery though all of us knew the ending. One rarely, after all, turns to the last page of a novel to find out the end. One follows instead the twists and turns, one stays with the immediacies. And so we did with her illness, like naive readers savoring every illusory effect.

America is a land of science and so realism is the preferred style in disease. No matter what personal mythologies or symbolism one brings to the situation, the principal scenes will be enacted in the context of science: the context of drugs, treatments, known facts, hypotheses, suppositions, deductions. In that context, my mother was not my mother, but P. "P. is 55 yr old woman, 2 prev. operations carcinoma rect." But in this algebra, my mother, reduced to P., was a meager quotient in proportion to her illness. Her illness was the focus of attack, treatment, speculation. It was irrelevant whether her suffering bent her in its shape, or if she were made for this suffering. That question belonged to the realm of symbolism.

What I wished to understand was how the disease which P. suffered related to my mother. Was the relation hidden but logical, as the dominant mode of medical realism would have us believe? Is the story a dry one of cause and effect? One thinks of the terrible statistics of cancer. If you have your bowels cut out, your leg amputated, your breast removed, "your" chances of survival are 30, 50, 60 per cent. Where do such figures come from? They speak a language of realism, but who can say to "you" what it means to have "your" leg amputated, "your" eye removed?

I do not believe a disease comes as punishment for a sin. Yet it seems possible that our bodies dream up their own elaborate pain, as though to emphasize, almost wittily, how elaborate our connection to life is, how difficult the untying of this knot that binds body to experience.

Although we always followed the story of P. and could recite quite clearly when called to the ironies and inevitabilities of P., that is not, finally, how we read my mother's illness. We read it rather as though it were a story written on our own flesh, as indeed it was. Our interest was dramaturgy, our resource digression; above all we wished to keep the story going; where we could not have hope, we at least hoped for suspense.

After a time though, and without our knowing it, my mother grew rather indifferent to the plot. She grew closer, in her affect, to P. If we had listened more carefully we might have noticed it sooner for she had developed her own vocabulary to distance herself. She seemed to stand apart from her body mentally. Her pain was all too real of course and yoked her brutally, but she foreshortened her view of it and did not attempt to string out the consequences.

I learned, for example, that tumors had so weakened her vertebrae there was a grave danger that a "rapid decompression" could crumble her spine like confectioner's sugar. This much I had drawn from her medical report in a sneaked glance. I wondered at first why they kept this from her. Isn't this something P. ought to know? Didn't anything written about P. belong to P.? Yet what was the use of her knowing it? No one falls on purpose.

It was precisely the kind of detail a story writer might use to create suspense. But the knowledge just made me feel worse. If her spine shattered, she would be completely paralyzed and then . . . I dwelled on it foolishly. At that point, death was so rich in endings: she had tumors in her bowels, her spine; she could die of morphine, chemotherapy, pneumonia . . .

My mother's vocabulary of illness was simple: "curable," "treatable," "setback." For many years, there had been talk of a cure. One is considered cured of a cancer if in three years following surgery, no new tumor appears. Indeed, my mother was pronounced "cured" a month before her secondary tumors surfaced. In the months that followed, as the facts of P. came to light, she began to shift terms, to say her illness was "treatable." She would say it quite solemnly, like an initiate repeating a pledge, "I know I am not curable, but I am treatable." She took comfort in the word, for though it hinted at an end, it also put that end off indefinitely.

Digression was a saving grace. She was happy so long as the doctors felt they could do something to her: treatments, surgeries, implantations. No matter whether it was for her. She willfully submitted to painful procedures, that at the most could buy her a little time, because they were part of the magic of the word "treatable." So long as she could pronounce herself "treatable" she could live with her illness from day to day, she could make plans, she could lie in a hospital bed on the cancer ward and talk of going out. She could put on her makeup each day, arrange her blasted hair, receive her visitors. And then one day, the last doctor told her he could do no more.

"Curable," "treatable," "setback"—these words helped her live from day to day. She did not elaborate them into a fiction, she held herself within their boundaries. She did not ask "a setback from what" or wonder aloud, at least, where she was going. She knew. She was far from unconscious. She was able to say, "I know I am going to die." One night I was talking to my parents about a house I might buy. I noticed that she excluded herself from this conversation. She grew silent, sat and stared into space in an oddly intense way. Because of the swelling of her cheeks, her eyes appeared closer together, like a hawk's fixed on its prey. She stared through my father and me, with a look of pain on her face that was metaphysical, gritting her teeth as though against an acceleration of time. She was falling away from us.

Perhaps a lack of knowledge or imagination of what goes on inside our bodies is a protective device. To see a man on the street with a finger missing unaccountably shames us. We imagine he has suffered obscenely or perhaps is capable of all sorts of crimes. Yet we do not speak of "internal mutilation."

My mother's illness was relatively hidden. Her original tumors had been in the bowels. The secondary tumors attacked her cerebellum, an organ she had never been aware of. The physical effects of those tumors did not frighten her because they were unimaginable. How to imagine an organ of the body as subtle in its functions as the cerebellum? How to map its pains or create a landscape for them? Too abstract, too small and grey. What did scare her were the spiritual effects. Because the cerebellum was part of the brain, she feared that she would lose her mind. I would reassure her constantly—I did not realize then how much I was reassuring myself—that the cerebellum was not the cerebrum, that it merely controlled motor functions and not thinking, that anyway the tumors there had been removed, and so on. She listened but it did not stick. It was pitiable. She would ask me, "What day is it? Is it Wednesday?" "No it is Thursday." Then, minutes later, again.

One day, her doctor took me aside. He had observed my mother standing in the examination room and she was, in his language, "confused, Parkinsonian, unable to initiate movement." She'd been trying to figure out how to put her skirt on over her shoes. He said, "Mrs. Kamenetz wasn't functioning like Mrs. Kamenetz." A strangely alienated phrase, the patient subtracted from herself, leaving what? No wonder my mother feared losing her mind; the disease had so ravaged her body, it was the last part of herself that was herself. The doctor suspended chemotherapy. "We don't want to save the patient's body at the expense of the patient."

They had been pumping powerful anti-tumor drugs through the plastic reservoir at the top of her head. But it turned out that they were draining too slowly. Instead of going down the spinal column they were resting on her brain, damaging the cerebrum. The chemotherapy had to be stopped; my mother was no longer "treatable."

They moved her out of the hospital to the Church Home Hospice. We felt hurt, as though Johns Hopkins Hospital had rejected us. We couldn't accept that from their point of view there was nothing they could do for her.

My mother understood. She knew what "hospice" meant. I was slower to understand. I rolled her around the hospice in a wheelchair, as I had at Johns Hopkins. But she had no interest in looking out the windows. Only once did she perk up. It so happened two of her neighbors were doctors there. We met them in the hallway. It was amazing to see my mother call up her old qualities of charm, to mask her face into a smile and banter as though at a party. We chatted for a few minutes until one had to go. He touched her hand and said, seriously, "Let me know if there's anything I can do for you." Her reply started as a joke, but she couldn't quite carry it off. "Make me well."

Her words were very sad. They bothered me too, because I saw she was able to speak quite well to these neighbors, yet for weeks she had barely spoken a word to me, or any of us in the family.

We were all pained by this. Because I felt guilty about

being in Mexico during her first operation, I tormented myself. I feared her silence hid a great anger.

I wished too, with all my heart, that I could make her well. But her silence chilled me. It was like a forewarning of her death. I was helpless before it.

11

on the meaning of no

A madman used to call me on the telephone. His words were often quite strange. But sometimes, after saying "hello" in a very small voice, he would remain silent. There was a magic in the silence, pulling from his end. I felt I was being sucked down through the holes in the mouthpiece, the connection between us left drifting.

The silence of mad people is very powerful. Perhaps they have succeeded where I have failed. They hear speech for what it is, a jumble of meaningless sounds.

It is a great miracle that words mean anything at all. I have tried very hard to hear English as no language. To hear it as music, as birdsong. But even birdsong has a human meaning since we call it song. A dog barks with human emotions, and a cat seems to howl with human pain. Floorboards groan, the wind whistles, streams laugh—we personify all sounds.

At times, I have abstracted myself from reading a book and then it seems extraordinary that this inert object should so hold my attention. As though I sat for hours with a stone in my lap or a leaf.

I have a friend who talks to herself. I hear her in her office, and the voice is deep and angry, not hers at all. It is the voice, I think, of her father, amplified as a child might hear it, and he is yelling at her, telling her what to do. And then there is another voice, soothing, but also exacting, repeating a schedule, a list of commands. This "scheduling voice" is also parental, perhaps it is the mother, reconciling the demands of the father, the abilities of the child.

One morning my daughter Anya woke in her crib—she was about six months old—and I heard from her room a burbling sound. She was shaping it into syllables, "bu-bu-bu-bu-BO." It was a musical phrase, what Robert Frost called a "sentence sound." And she would laugh and do it again.

Then she learned NO. It was a lovely thing, not the flat curt No of superiors, authorities. Her *no* was a song—large, airy, expansive, hovering above her like a rich purple-black flag: N-A-A-O-O-U-H-U-H.

You could tell how she loved to say it, the way she inserted air into it and let it flutter awhile, billowing with her breath, so what unfurled as a black flag of anarchy spread a dark sky over the earth, a universe of stars and planets, all the things out there that she refused to be, so she could be herself instead.

Language makes us crazy by making us desire what isn't here. We can never have as purely as we can say. That is why the two-year-old maintains her rights of first refusal, her NAAOOUHUH.

No was not her first word. Like many babies, her first word was *ball*. Ball doesn't symbolize the world by its shape. It is the world. The first moiety excluded, expulsed—and everything else is ball, ball. In the supermarket she pointed to a head of lettuce—ball. An apple, an orange, my head, a lamp—all ball. And everything else was not ball. So her world was divided, not into darkness and light, but ball and not-ball.

Then frustration. Out of not-ball emerged *no*. Soon after

no came *Mommy* and *Daddy*. Anya sat sometimes in a corner of our bedroom, chanting, Mommy, Daddy, Mommy, Daddy. She was putting her world in order. She realized that we were not her and that mommy was not daddy. Now she knew her name. It was the same name we told her when she wanted what we couldn't give. It is the name for everything desirable, mysterious, and dangerous. Her name was NO.

She loved to say it. Do you want to eat? No. Do you want to get dressed? No. Do you want to go to sleep? No. (She didn't even know how to say yes.) Do you want to go to Charles's? No. Do you want *not* to go to Charles's? No. We thought we had her trapped. But No knows no metaphysical corners. No is not a simple refusal. It is a place of creation. And so she practiced it by herself. Nobody had asked her any questions, but still she sang it, No, NO, NOOO. She was building a world of it.

All my life I too have been learning the meaning of the word No. Like Anya, I have built a world of it. I believe that my mother's strange secrecy, her silence, is what got me interested in poetry. For poetry is the meaning of the word No.

Everything absent inspires poetry. Everything absent inspires new names. That is why poets court absence. The most beautiful rose, Mallarmé wrote, is the rose absent from all bouquets.

Keats's negative capability describes a mind with no names in it, "no irritable reaching after fact or reason" except what comes to mind. When something comes to mind, there is no overtone of ego or possession, no "I thought" or "my idea." It came to mind. From where? From nowhere, from nothing, from no.

Robert Duncan in his poem "Often I am Permitted to Return to a Meadow," speaks of "a place of first permission / everlasting omen of what is," speaks of a field that is both a child's meadow and a field of language: a dream "whose secret we see in a children's game of ring a round of roses told."

The child discovers the meadow, the "place of first permission," through his no. The poet returns to this place of negation, of negative capability, in order to begin the round again.

Andrei Codrescu, the poet, was depressed when one of his books came out. Why? I asked him. Because books are tombs, he said. Once a book is written, it is only a marker of where language had once been alive. That is why Mallarmé called so many of his poems "tombeaus." They are tombs of pure language. Non-language, the unconditional, has left these tombs behind as monuments. Once a spirit passed through here, the words seem to say, but now only, *çi-gît*, here lies . . .

It follows that the proper etiquette for reading poetry is learned by visiting graves. Many poets have stood before Apollinaire's tomb at Père Lachaise and read the calligramme carved on the stone: *Mon coeur comme une flamme renversée*. My heart like an upside down flame.

What is the proper feeling to bring to the graveyard, and to the poem? One must again turn the flame upside down. A grave is sacred, it was once believed, because the spirits of the dead reside there. No, the spirits are smuggled into the cemetery by the visitors. They bring them, along with their fresh flowers (that soon fade) and their ancient prayers (quickly mumbled). They carry the spirits of the dead back to their graves, perhaps to have done with them.

Turning the flame upside down turns the heart rightside up. It puts the flame back inside the heart. It puts disturbance back inside the language, the disturbance of the reader's confusion beating inside the dead language of the writer. Then, for a moment, the flame will seem to flicker, "a disturbance of words within words" (Robert Duncan).

When my mother could not move without great pain, she thought to hide her speech. Her silence then was like a return to the conditions of my early childhood. I never thought she would go into death that way, refusing to talk. I was even driven to ask her, "What are you thinking?" She said, "I'm not thinking."

Towards the end, she refused medication. The nurse gave her pills for pain and she'd hold them at the tips of her trembling fingers, as if to say, "What do they want me to take now?" In the end, they had to chop the pills into her mush. But she wouldn't eat either.

She made no sign when we entered or left. Only now and then a tear seemed to come from a corner of her eyes, her great open eyes, dark brown, which stared without blinking at an empty spot on the wall. We rubbed her hands with lanolin, but afterwards, she would drop them like clumsy objects; we moistened her lips with lemon glycerine, we read to her from the newspaper. She did not respond.

I don't know what words we expected from our mother before she died. I don't know if we imagined some profound speech, some formal message. Or simply, like little children, we were terrified, guilty and afraid, as we had been so many years ago, before her great rages.

Our game was to guess at the meaning of her silence, to weigh this non-speech and feel its contours. Because she was dying, her silence had an artistic quality. We felt, as we often do before a tombstone, or a poem, that it must mean something more.

At the very end, my mother was stepping back to a pre-language, a babble. A few times in coma, I heard her murmur, "Grandfather, grandfather . . ." She had the voice of a child then, a very clear voice like a sparrow's song.

My mother died the year Anya was born. And so the

paths of their lives formed an X. As one went into silence, the other came out of it, their paths crossing through the same point. The point of silence, the point of No. One calling out like a little girl, "Grandfather, grandfather." The other screaming, No.

Why didn't my mother speak to us? I think she felt our fear and knew we were far too fragile for anything she might have to say. She was guarding a great power. Her no was not a black flag of anarchy, but a seal of refusal. It held us captive. We wanted to make it speak, to tell us more. In my bewilderment, I imagined all sorts of mysteries.

Only two days before she died, we ate a last "meal" in the hospice together. Her face, veined and rouged, hair short grey fuzz, a yellow plastic bubble on her skull. My father and I wheeled her through the cafeteria line. She had a grey plastic tray in front of her: jello, tea, crackers. She wouldn't eat. Neither could we. A middle-aged woman at the next table was staring at her. My mother straightened up in her chair.

"What are you staring at?" she whispered. Her throat was hoarse. I was astonished that my mother spoke. Why was she wasting words on this total stranger when she would not speak to us?

"Oh, I am not staring . . . I thought I recognized you . . . don't I know you?"

"NO!"

The woman backed away like a crab. The cafeteria was hushed: no fork clatter, no banging of trays. In that terrible *no*, we had been picked up and whirled to a place of dark anger.

The evening my mother died, we all went back to the house, sat in the living room near the piano. Our rabbi came, and we found out that during that time of silence she had spoken quite clearly to him, and at length.

"What did she say to you, rabbi?"

"She said she was very afraid that after she died, her family would not stay together."

At the time I found it touching that my mother had this last ambition. She had tried to keep us together even after she knew her own case was utterly hopeless. But her strategy seemed odd. True, her silence succeeded in drawing us together more than any words might have. But I could not help but feel the anger behind the gesture. She neither forgave nor asked forgiveness. It was a deliberate separation. She was dying and her silence was negating us. Even as the rabbi spoke, and even, in my grief, as I accepted his explanation, I still brooded.

The rabbi asked us how we would describe our mother, something he could use in his eulogy. It was up to me to speak.

"Tell them," I said, "she was fierce."

12

last words

There is very little left to avoid, only one thing left to tell: how my mother died. I find in my notebooks the following entry, two weeks before her death:

Sunday April 13:
Early that morning, around 9 stayed til 2. She was sitting in her chair, *gorked out*, soft-boiled egg spilled on her gown.

She had been administered an overdose of a painkiller. She was sitting upright, or rather, her body was slanted against the high-backed wheelchair, for "sitting" implies a certain activity of the will. In front of her was a tray with toast and soft boiled egg. Her right hand hung to one side, clutching a fork; the egg yolk dribbled in a chain from her chin to the gown. She had stopped in mid-bite, as in a silly film where time is frozen for some of the characters and others walk about studying them. I thought she had died. But her chest was moving slightly.

I was stunned by the sight, a rehearsal of her death. But then I went home to my notebook. I could not forget the egg yellow. It was like a strange detail of an obsessed writing that suddenly looms larger than it should. No longer subordinated to the planification of realism (for realism is a kind of literary city-planning), such details trip up the narrative, like the series of shocks in a Poe tale.

The coldness of death summons the chill of intellect. A distance sets in. The young writer notes. The young doctor jokes.

I first saw a dead body in the dissection room at Johns Hopkins. My friend, Marc, a beginning medical student, learned anatomy there. My only visit—to meet Marc for lunch—left me with an unappetizing impression: corpse fat on corpse flesh, like chicken fat smeared on old meat.

The dissection room was full of comic relief. Various medical students were willing to swear that in the alley behind the lab lay wooden crates stamped PRODUCT OF INDIA. A sandwich would sometimes wind up inside a body cavity. One student rigged a string to his cadaver's penis and slung it over the light fixture. He greeted his partner with an erection. The occasion for every joke was "Joe" the stiff, the ultimate straight man.

Two years later, Marc was making his first hospital rounds. One day he walked into a room and greeted his patient, before seeing she was dead. He felt closed in. He forced open the window, stuck his head out and vomited down the air shaft.

Eventually, his stomach hardened. The joking from the cadaver room found its way to the hospital wards. In the young doctors' slang, a semi-comatose patient became a "G.O.R.K." Is she alive or dead? God Only Really Knows.

A gork might rest for weeks or months supported by an IV. The nursing staff would have to move her body to prevent bedsores, exercise her limbs, change her bedpans. The gorks could not talk, or would not. They just lay there. When a gork died, she "gave the Q-sign"—her tongue fell out of the corner of her mouth. But Q was also the abbreviation of a feeling.

The day I saw my mother "gorked out," a cold part of me

recorded something particular in a notebook: "soft-boiled eggs spilled on her gown." It is a trick of realism to accumulate such details.

Indigestible moments underlie Poe's writing. They show the horror of immobility, of the crossing from life to death. Poe's Monsieur Valdemar, for instance, is hypnotized on his deathbed. Suspended in a trance-induced coma, he is literature's first gork. The conception of the tale is startling enough. But the detail that has haunted readers is Valdemar's voice. It "impressed me" says the narrator ". . . as gelatinous or glutinous matters impress the sense of touch."

The disgusting voice of the gork is the undertone of an obsessed writing, a writing unable to fully revive a memory or to let it die. It is not just Monsieur Valdemar, but pained memory itself that cries out, "For God's sake!—quick!—quick—put me to sleep—or quick!—waken me!—quick!—*I say to you that I am dead.*"

After my mother died, I was haunted by dreams. Painful memory spoke to me in her form. In the power of her last moment, I had hoped to be released. I found myself instead hypnotized, perpetually suspended in my feeling. I had a compulsion to write. Reason wanted to kill this emotion, emotion wanted to sustain the memory. The result was digression, a writing that moved back and forth between memory and meditation, a haunting that thought alone could not cure.

When I was a student a retired German professor hired me to help translate his poetry. He was a very sentimental poet, but that was God's fault. Fighting for the Kaiser in World War I, he had had a religious experience in the midst of the battle of Verdun. Terrified by the dying all around him, he sank to his knees and prayed to God, "Save me and I will dedicate my life to You."

He was spared. And so he carried with him for the next

fifty years a religious obsession that bordered on delusion. He believed, for instance, that he had immense spiritual powers, could see into the future and change people's lives. He was obsessed with health food and vitamins. He used to make awful herbal soups, bouillons with green and brown flecks floating on their greasy surface.

His diet did him some good. At seventy, he had great energy and vitality. He wore tight hiking shorts. His legs and arms were muscular, but the skin on his forehead was dry and shiny, pressed against his skull, giving him a cadaverous look. Death was on his mind constantly, death and Oral Roberts, whom he wrote, hoping to become a minister in his old age and testify about the effect of God on his life, the battlefield promise and revelation.

Whenever I entered his house, he would bring me into his kitchen and make me drink his bouillon. Frequently, he told me the story of his friend, an elderly woman who had died in her home and whose body had not been found for a week. Her dogs, desperately hungry, had eaten off her leg.

The old man's fear of death was hideous, enormous. It had dominated his whole life from the battlefield to the present. I could taste it in his bouillon, a deadly soup in which the details of his life were broken down into protein and salt. He saw his body, abandoned, eaten away by death. He had hired me to find him when he died. He wanted me to help him, not just to translate his poetry, but to translate his death away from the unspeakable.

I could not help him, just as I could not help my mother. At her death, I was listening to her last words, still waiting for some message from her.

I had forced myself to be there, as I had been through the last stages of her illness. Even though she would no longer speak, I had to touch the quality of that silence. As though I were a child again, I was hanging on her last words, hoping they would explain everything that hurt me.

There is a great mythology about "last words." Certainly death is a great framing device, but I am very suspicious, particularly of writers and their last words. They give their death a finished quality. Doesn't this presumption deprive ordinary people of the equality of death?

My mother's last words seem sentimental. She spared us any additional pain. She gave us at the end a sign that all would be well. We needed that badly.

There was an awful pump in her room, a contraption that smelled of the nineteenth century, a vacuum jar with rubber tubes, a piston that moved lugubriously up and down inside the vacuum with an expiring sound. I will never forget its sad gelatinous quivering. My mother's throat was full of phlegm, and there was white mold growing on her tongue and gums from lack of eating. The nurse would stick the tube down her throat to try to draw up the phlegm. I made her stop. The sound of the pump was too much to bear. It disturbed my mother in her sleep.

She died to easy listening. Because life is often perfectly ironic, the call letters of the station were WLIF, "the music of your life." I was even annoyed with her for it and thought of changing the station.

The other sound in the room was a death rattle. Harsh, rasping. It had an odor of salt about it, if a sound can have an odor. Her voice was becoming elemental, and mucous as the sea.

Then her eyelids fluttered and she lifted her head from the pillow. Her breath quieted. My father leaned forward and said her name with great happiness. I think he believed she was coming out of the coma. Indeed, her eyes opened, she looked directly into his with full consciousness. She spoke her last words very distinctly, in tones that seemed humanly distant from the grotesque death rattle. And then she was gone.

One had the sensation of the spirit leaving her body with the voice, and the body cast off like so many used clothes.

I've often wondered, since, how much she was aware even in coma. A few minutes before she died, I had persuaded my father to break off our vigil and go downstairs for a Coke. It seemed useless to sit since the nurse had told us she might remain in coma for days. My father wanted to wait, though, until exactly five o'clock, when the shift changed. Then the phone rang, my sister calling. At the sound, my mother stirred.

There we were: my father, my sister, and I, together at the same moment. And my brothers and other sister were thinking of her too. As though she pulled the threads connecting her to all of us, at once. She moved, my sister spoke of her, my father leaned forward, and all of us were united in one gesture, her last.

My mother had cut herself off from her past, until her sister cried at her grave, "You were never there when I needed you." Now I have come, too late, to answer that cry. I have brought back the secrets of her childhood and asked to understand her strange, fierce will.

She believed she could do anything. This was her flaw. She could not overcome her illness with pride. The pattern has the optimism of tragedy. After the sufferings of the hero, something survives in the spirit.

She had broken with me, told my brother coldly enough, she had given up on me. And in the last weeks of her life, though she spoke to strangers, she turned her sister away, and she did not speak to her children.

I had done the same to her. In my turmoil and rebellion, I had fled from one end of the country to the other, hoping to put enough distance between us so I could be myself. In an agony of rebirth, I tore myself from her, told her I hated her, and made her grieve.

And yet I was drawn back to her. In the last year of her life, I played my old role as favorite son. I witnessed her dying, though with what strange mixture of genuine grief and triumph at her helplessness, I can't fully know. The injuries and wrongs on both sides were never fully acknowledged, never fully expressed.

She was theatrical to the end. She knew how to be haunting. She knew the power of guilt. The night she came off her deathbed to hear the cantata, she showed everyone the enormous power of her will, her grim version of stage presence. She believed she could do anything.

How she dreamed of controlling me. How she wished I would always remain her sunshine boy. Deep in her heart, she did not imagine any of her children could grow up, be married, have a life of his own. And she did it all in the name of love.

She said "love" in that last sad room. Spirit and body were going in opposite directions, the voice and the spirit rising up, lifting her into the air, and with the sensation of shooting right through the top of her head as she expired. Then her body fell back in a heap.

Out of her silence, and her animal slumber, she spoke one last time, unforgettably. She said, "I love you."

Yet I have come to wonder what she meant by love. A love that never set me free, a love that bound my voice to hers in confusion. Even in my most powerful dreams I could not tell whose voice was speaking, hers or mine. Willful to the end, she had withheld her speech from us until the last possible moment, as if sure of her effect. Her voice, though the voice of a gork, was a human performance. Her dying words were a triumph. They hold me still in their grip. Because, as she spoke them, she seemed very much alive.

A few months after she died, I had the dream in which she told me that the events I thought unrelated were connected in the spirit, part of a single motion, like a wave through water. It was the dream that told me I might make a whole story from the scattered moments of her life.

I see now I have been mistaken about the origin of that dream. It was not our walk in the hospice garden, not the white tulips. The dream grew from her last gesture, her last words. And a voice that spoke from a dying body, from beyond life.

Now in the wake of that dream, word after word has risen and fallen, broken and receded. This book is one wave, her legacy and her will.